CONVICTIONS

A woman political prisoner remembers

Jean Middleton

Ravan Press

First published in 1998 by
Ravan Press
PO Box 145
Randburg
2125

© Jean Middleton

ISBN 0 86975 474 2

Typesetting and design: Positive Proof cc
Cover design: Concept Creations and Design cc
Printed by: Creda Communications

Our thanks to the following who supplied the photographs: Sheila
Weinberg, Ann Nicholson and Gerhard Jahn. In a few cases we
were not able to locate the copyright holder. If brought to our
attention, we would be pleased to rectify this in a future impression.

Biographical Note

Jean Middleton was born and raised in Durban, and went to university in Pietermaritzburg. She then went to London, and spent two years there, before returning to Natal, where she taught at technical colleges and high schools, before moving to Johannesburg to teach. She became involved in anti-apartheid politics, and was arrested and detained in 1964. After nearly a year in detention and awaiting trial, she was sentenced to three more years, in the trial of Bram Fischer and fourteen others.

After her release, placed under restrictions that made it impossible for her to earn a living, she returned to London, where she became active in the Anti-Apartheid Movement, and the National Union of Teachers, travelled to Germany, Bulgaria, Greece, Cyprus and the then Soviet Union. For the last seven years of her stay overseas, she worked for *Sechaba,* the journal of the ANC.

Jean returned to South Africa in 1991, lived in Durban for four years and then moved to Johannesburg. She was editor of the South African Communist Party paper, *Umsebenzi,* for two and a half years, and has been writing for the London *Morning Star.*

Dedication

This book is dedicated to all those who visited political prisoners, and otherwise cared for and comforted them, during the years of apartheid.

Contents

CHAPTER 1

Arrest

Early one morning in 1964, it happened to me, as it happened to thousands of others during the apartheid years: I was woken by a violent rapping on the door. It was twenty to seven, midwinter in Johannesburg, cold and still dark. I got out of bed and went into the bathroom, where the window opened on to the landing outside the flat. I called, "Who's there?" though I knew it must be the security police.

Apart from a few banned books, all I had at the time that might have been interesting or useful to them was a clandestinely produced document about the campaign for sanctions against South Africa, that was then being set up overseas. I was supposed to pass the document on for others to read, but this was the time to get rid of it. As I got ready to go to the door, I put it down the lavatory.

Of course, the police knew about this method of destroying evidence and, when they heard the lavatory flush, they forced my door at once, reaching the bathroom before I had got into the second sleeve of my dressing gown. They were furiously annoyed, and showed it by treating me roughly. The officer in charge of the arrest, a huge man, going to seed but still powerful, took me by the shoulders and threw me across the room with such force that I landed heavily on a sofa against the opposite wall. They ran past into the bathroom to get to whatever I had put down the drain, but it had gone.

They refused to produce a search warrant or, later, a warrant for my arrest. I lived alone, so if they broke or bent the law in their treatment of me there would be no witnesses to embarrass them in the future. They refused to produce identity cards, so it was impossible to find out names or ranks. Security branch men avoided giving such details whenever they could. Months later, I recognised the man in charge, in a newspaper photograph: he was Colonel Fred van Niekerk, boss of the security branch in Pretoria. I have often wondered how many prisoners he lost his temper with, in closed interrogation rooms.

The three of them searched my one-roomed flat for over three hours, crowding the tiny place. I knew I should watch them closely, in case they tried to plant evidence, but it was impossible to watch all three at once and, in any case, in a court of law, it would be no more than my word against theirs. There was nothing for me to do but sit on the bed and look on. It was Friday, my day for dyeing my eyebrows and eyelashes, so I got out the little bottles and brushes, and a hand mirror, and, for part of the time, occupied myself that way. My face in the mirror was an unpleasant, pasty colour.

I went to the kitchen and made coffee, but only one cup, for myself. In those days, political activists sometimes offered tea or coffee to the detectives who came to raid – perhaps to distract them, perhaps to sweeten them up, perhaps as a way of demonstrating who held the moral high ground – but the behaviour these men had shown me had done nothing to make me want to give them any refreshment. I needed that coffee, but it was a mistake, all the same. I was trying to appear cool, unafraid, impervious to bullying, but the clattering of the cup in the saucer betrayed how I was shaking. After that, I folded my arms tightly, to keep my hands still.

At a quarter to nine, while they were still going through my clothes, reading papers, and paging through books on the shelves, they let me make a telephone call to say I wouldn't be coming to work. That was when they told me I was being detained in terms of the ninety-day detention law that, in those days, provided for detention and interrogation without trial. In practice, it meant indefinite detention at the whim of the security police, who sometimes released their prisoners before the ninety-day period was up, sometimes held them for the full ninety days and then immediately rearrested them for another period.

It was the last day of the school term. The standard nine and matric students had written their mid-year examinations, and the scripts were to be marked during the July holidays. It was clear that the English scripts weren't going to be marked by me.

When I made my call, I asked to speak to Norman Levy, who was vice-principal of the private college where I was teaching then. He wasn't there. I was put on to someone else, who, when I explained what was happening, said, "What? You too?" Standing beside me, Van Niekerk said, with heavy sarcasm, "I wonder why Norman Levy isn't there," and I knew then that Norman was being arrested too, and almost certainly others as well. We had heard rumours that there was to be a general sweep of activists and, though I didn't know it at the time, people all over the country were being taken from their homes that morning, in a co-ordinated police operation.

Those were the worst of times, the darkest days of repression. Nelson Mandela and the others had been sentenced to life imprisonment three weeks before. Innumerable other trials had been taking place throughout the country, over the past three years. People had been tried singly and in groups; in supreme courts, regional courts, magistrates' courts, sometimes in the cells below the courts. They had been gaoled for membership of banned organisations, possession of banned literature, attempting to cross the border, helping, or attempting to help, others cross it; recruiting, or being recruited, for military training; for sabotage of government installations, attempted sabotage. Some had even been tried, charged and gaoled for doing no more than form groups to discuss sabotage.

Under the ninety-day detention law, the police held their prisoners in solitary confinement and usually incommunicado, and it was well known that they often used physical torture to get information. Some prisoners had already died in detention. Some who had turned in detention, and some who had been police spies all along, had given evidence against those who were being tried. Others, who had been brought from solitary cells straight to the witness box, and had refused to give evidence, were serving sentences for that principled and courageous refusal.

I had known I was likely to be arrested. Three or four men had been standing at the end of my street for days, apparently doing nothing but look under the bonnet of a car. They were watching the front entrance of the block of flats where I lived but, presumably because they knew I didn't have a car, they seemed not to have posted anyone to watch the alleyway at the back, where the entrances to the basement car parks were. When I wanted to avoid being observed, I took the lift down to the basement, went out by that way, on foot, crossed the alleyway, passed through another basement, and emerged from the front entrance of another block of flats in another street.

In spite of my precautions, I had been followed two nights before, when Ann Nicholson and I took a bus up Hospital Hill. A man who certainly hadn't been waiting at the bus-stop suddenly appeared from the shadows under the trees outside the hospital, and climbed on after us. I was struck by the spontaneous look of pleased recognition he gave us, almost as if he were greeting old acquaintances. We didn't know him, but he looked as if he knew us. We had been going to a meeting but decided against it; rode on the bus as far as Rosebank, looked into a few shop windows, and caught another bus back to Hillbrow.

I had kept the sanctions document with me at all times, with the idea of being able to dispose of it at a moment's notice. I had been prepared to eat it, if need be. I knew that would be difficult because I'd eaten a piece of paper once before, to prevent its falling into the hands of the police. It had been quite a small piece of paper, but I'd found it hard to get down.

The arrival of the security men, therefore, wasn't a surprise, though it was frightening. That morning, I didn't stop shaking for three hours. I told myself that what was happening would have been all in the day's work for a heroine of the French Resistance in World War Two, or the Algerian war of independence, but that didn't help.

When, at last, the search was over, they told me I could get dressed and pack my bag for prison. One of the younger policemen said I should go into the bathroom; that there was no need for me to get dressed in front of them. He spoke with studied insolence, and all I could do was glare back at him without replying. Once I was in the bathroom, I think delayed shock must have set in because, for a minute or two, I found I couldn't stand. I knelt by the side of the bath, with my head on my folded arms, till I felt better. It was clear I didn't shape up to my ideas of what a heroine of the revolution should be like, but I tried to retrieve all the strength I could, and hoped I was looking calm, dignified and defiant when I came out, dressed and carrying my bag.

Outside the flat, there was a fourth man, who must have been there all the time, no doubt in case I made a dash for it. Surrounded by these detectives, I got into the lift, walking as steadily as I could on trembling knees. Outside the building, there was a car waiting at the kerb. I never saw the inside of that flat again.

They dropped the two younger men off in town, and then made for the road to Pretoria. One of them told me, "You'll soon be singing like a canary," and they then spent the rest of the time chatting to each other in Afrikaans about a rugby game they'd watched. As we drove through the dry winter veld, I wondered when I'd come back that way.

CHAPTER 2

Bannings, restrictions and growing oppression

I had been active for about eight years in what later came to be called the South African "democratic movement". Then, it was generally known as the "Congress movement", because it was based on the alliance between the African National Congress and the Indian Congress. Sometimes we referred to it as "the left movement" or simply "the movement". I'd joined the multi-racial Liberal Party when it was first formed, but grew dissatisfied because its franchise policy included a property qualification, which would have the effect of excluding the majority of people in South Africa. Through a small discussion group organised by the local branch of the Natal Indian Congress in Pieter-maritzburg, I drew closer to the Congresses, whose policies were for non-racism and universal franchise.

The Congress alliance was growing. The Coloured People's Congress was added, and the South African Congress of Trade Unions. The Congress of Democrats, (known as COD), was formed in the early nineteen-fifties, as a political home for whites who supported Congress policies, and was part of the Congress Alliance. It had no branch in Pietermaritzburg but, when I moved to Durban, I joined the branch there. When I moved again, this time to Johannesburg, I continued as a member, and later served on the national propaganda committee, and on the national executive committee.

Our task was to reach out to whites, to inform them of Congress policies of non-racism. We were a small organisation, but vociferous. We condemned the evils of apartheid, declared our support for equal rights and universal suffrage, asserted the need for a non-racist, equitable society. Morally, it was all unexceptionable stuff but, under apartheid, morality and legality had little to do with each other, and we had a great deal of unwelcome attention from the police, who sometimes raided meetings, and seized minutes and other documents. We remained open and public, but we had to keep our documents safe, and take care that only members knew when and where our meetings were to be held.

It was difficult to gain expression for our point of view, for the press was reluctant to print any articles, even letters, of any but the mildest protest. Many whites were hostile to what we had to say, many were apathetic, some were sympathetic but afraid of police reprisals, and here the danger was real. The public meetings we tried to call were nothing like the huge rallies the ANC held in black townships; as a rule, the only people who came to our meetings were ourselves and representatives of the security police. Journals like *Liberation* and *Fighting Talk* ceased to appear when it became too difficult to produce them any longer. Cyclostyled journals, sent anonymously to mailing lists, appeared briefly from time to time but, more and more, our messages to the public were conveyed in the form of leaflets which we gave out in the street, placards which we held on demonstrations, posters which we put up where we could, small adhesive flyposters (which we called "stickers") and graffiti.

In the earlier days, the evenings when we put up posters and stickers, and painted slogans, had been light-hearted and sociable. We met at someone's house, had coffee, collected our posters and pots of paste, or stickers, or brushes and tins of paint, and went off in twos and threes. In the early sixties, the Sabotage Act changed all that, for, though it was directed more specifically against organisations engaged in armed struggle, it affected all forms of political activity, including this one. Under the Act, we faced a penalty of eighteen months' imprisonment, a year of which was usually suspended, for putting out our messages of justice and democracy.

We were slow in responding to the new situation, and there was one calamitous slogan-painting evening when nearly all those taking part were arrested. We were to feel its repercussions for some time to come, but the first result was that Mollie Anderson, Pixie Benjamin, Eve Hall and Mary Turok, all strong activists, were sentenced to an effective six months' imprisonment. I missed the whole affair, for I was at a parent-teacher meeting. I'd intended to help paint slogans afterwards, and had gone out with espadrilles and old cotton trousers rolled up in my bag, but the meeting finished after eleven, much later than anyone expected, and I went straight home.

After that, we organised more tightly, into groups we called "volunteer" groups, named after the "volunteers" of the Congress-led Defiance Campaign of the early fifties.

The Suppression of Communism Act had been passed in 1950, with the express purpose of banning the Communist Party. Ten years later, it was used again to ban the ANC and, again, in 1962, to ban the Congress of Democrats. However, even before the banning of the ANC and the COD, being an active member of one of the Congress organisations carried with it the danger of a prison sentence, or the danger of being imprisoned without trial, as thousands of activists had been during the State of Emergency the government imposed after the Sharpeville massacre in 1960.

After organisations were banned, former members known to the police were exposed to further harassment: they were "named" in lists that were published in the Government Gazette. There weren't many restrictions connected with the status of being "named" or "listed", but it meant police surveillance, and a greater danger of being imprisoned without trial; ten years after the Communist Party had been banned, all "named" former members had been among those detained during the 1960 State of Emergency. It could also create difficulties at work, for employers (nearly all white in those days) tended to avoid taking on people who attracted the attention of the police, and feared suspicion might fall on them as well.

Individuals, as well as organisations, faced the danger of being banned, which was much more serious than being "named", and was a way of neutralising activists against whom there was no evidence that would stand up in court. Later, a number of members of the Liberal Party were banned as well.

The documents that constituted banning orders were signed by the Minister of Justice, the police served them on the designated people, and there was no appeal. Banned people were forbidden to leave the magisterial districts they lived in, except with special permission from the chief magistrate. They were not allowed to communicate in any way with other banned people, or with "named" people. They could not enter the premises of any factory or any educational institution. Nothing they wrote or said could be published. They were also forbidden to go to any meetings. At first, most of them continued to attend committee meetings, held in living rooms and disguised as tea parties, until further legislation barred them from gatherings altogether. It was never made clear exactly how many people constituted a gathering in the law – two? three? – and no one was willing to risk a gaol sentence by testing the law in court.

Later, new legislation added another clause to banning orders: a house arrest clause. Some orders specified twenty-four-hour house arrest, which confined the victim to his or her home. The local chief magistrate had the power to lift or modify the rules, temporarily, but consent was difficult to get, and application procedures were cumbersome. Alternatively, there was twelve-hour house arrest, from six or seven in the morning till six at night, with full twenty-four-hour confinement over weekends and public holidays. This allowed people to earn their living, but gave no space for social life, for they were forbidden to have visitors in their homes. Being placed under these restrictions drove a number of people to leave the country, for they had been politically neutralised and felt they would accomplish nothing by remaining in South Africa to face intolerably lonely lives.

The spirited Helen Joseph, a British woman, who had adopted South Africa as her country, and had been a central figure in the Women's Federation and the campaign against passes for African women, was one of the first to be restricted in this way. She kept her job during the week, but evenings and weekends were solitary and tedious because she lived alone. She used to complain of being persecuted by a security policeman called Viviers, who sometimes knocked on her door late at night, demanding to search the premises for visitors. During weekends, some of us used to stand on the pavement outside her house and chat for a while over the garden fence, for the law couldn't prevent that. Helen never left the country. Stubborn, defiant, courageous, and full of indignation against injustice, she remained, through re-imposed restrictions, till the end of her life, which came soon after South Africa began to change and her restrictions fell away.

Over the years, numbers of activists were served with banning orders that removed them from open political work. Towards the mid-sixties, one or two of those who were banned were very young and inexperienced indeed, and the police must have known this. Their intention must have been to intimidate others but, in spite of intimidation, there were always a few more young, enthusiastic, idealistic recruits coming up.

As time passed, a series of laws enabled the police to ignore the rule of *habeas corpus* when they chose. To emergency regulations, which the government could invoke at any time, were added laws providing for imprisonment without trial: first for twelve days, then for ninety days, then for one hundred and eighty days. The purpose of these detentions was openly stated: it was to interrogate, and get information.

The Congress of Democrats had first been formed as an organisation where white communists and non-communists could stand together on a political platform of democratic principles. In practice though, by the time the organisation was banned and dissolved, most of its members had been recruited into the underground Communist Party. I had been recruited towards the end of 1960.

The dissolution of the organisation left some of the younger members in limbo, with no political home. Many of them, full of indignation and courage, wanted the COD to go underground, as the Communist Party and the ANC had done. So angry and rebellious were they, that the national executive committee of the COD called in Walter Sisulu to speak to them. Then, as later, he was one of the most respected of the ANC leaders, and they accepted what he told them. He explained that there was no possibility of an underground COD, for if it were to announce its existence, the police would know exactly whom to pick up, almost to the last member. For the time being, we had to keep the "volunteer" groups going.

By 1962, a good deal of the opposition to the Pretoria government was being organised underground, by three illegal organisations: the Communist Party, the African National Congress and the new military organisation, Umkhonto we Sizwe, which came to be generally known as MK. Their rules were strict: membership and group organisation were closely guarded secrets, and their meetings clandestine. Banned people took part, though there was a risk.

The central event of this period was the arrest of Walter Sisulu and other leaders of the liberation movement, in July 1963. Tipped off by someone who had given information in detention, the police mounted a huge, surprise raid on Liliesleaf Farm, in Rivonia, near Johannesburg. It had been used as a safe house, a clandestine hiding-place, for underground activists, and for secret documents and other equipment, and when the police arrived, a number of people had gathered there for a meeting. The police made a tremendous haul, of both activists and documents. The capture of Sisulu was particularly important, as he had been in hiding for some time. Nelson Mandela wasn't there, for he had already been captured, and was serving a gaol sentence. It was a triumph for the police, and a serious setback for the liberation movement.

The news came out the next day, through a series of extra editions published by the newspapers, for there was no television in South Africa then, and South African radio was well-known as a poor conveyor of news. I remember well that devastating day. It was during the school holidays. I was sitting with a friend on the balcony of a cafe in Hillbrow, overlooking the street, and each time we saw a new edition arrive on the street below, we went down and bought it.

All those arrested were put into detention. The central figures, those who were present at the meeting, were brought to court towards the end of the year, charged with planning sabotage. Nelson Mandela was brought to be charged with them. The trial came to be known as the Rivonia trial, and it was the most famous of all the political trials of those days, making international headlines. There was a possibility of the death penalty, because the accused had been discussing military action as a means of overthrowing the state. Verdict and sentence came in June 1964, and only Lionel Bernstein, known as Rusty, was acquitted. Everyone knows the rest of the story: the others were given life sentences, and lived to be released from prison after twenty-six years.

People of all cultures and races were engaged in the underground political work but, though non-racism was the principle we were all struggling for, racially mixed meetings were difficult to hold, even under legal conditions, and certainly in secret, because they attracted attention from people round about. Much of the danger was from unfriendly whites, who had been known to call the police to say they had seen blacks and whites going together into the same house. Underground groups were based on residential areas wherever possible, and therefore were, of necessity, race-based. I lived in a white area, and nearly all the people I worked with were white, which is why the story I have to tell about my own experiences is almost entirely about whites.

However hard we tried though, few of us in illegal work then were to last very long in that transitional period between open and covert political activity. This went for the whole district of Johannesburg, and for all districts throughout the country. One problem was, of course, our inexperience in underground work; even some older, more experienced people, who had had their political beginnings in the days of the legal Party, found it difficult to keep to the new rules and think in the new way. Most important was the fact that we were all known to the police, and many of us to the public as well.

The first generation of underground activists had to be people who had previously engaged in open work. There was no alternative; no one else had the political experience, nor the necessary experience in organising. People who were committed to what we stood for, but who were not well known to the police, were very few, especially among whites, and they were valuable. As for the rest of us, the police simply had to follow the same people they had been keeping an eye on for years.

I was regarded as not being very well known, yet I had been arrested twice: at a demonstration in Pietermaritzburg in 1956, and later, putting up stickers in Johannesburg in 1961. I had been visited at school by the security branch, who had taken me home to search my flat. Six months before my arrest, because of my politics in general and this visit in particular, I had lost my job at the large private high school where I had taught for five years. I was lucky that Norman had hired me for the private college.

CHAPTER 3

Illegal work, and some of the people who did it

Recruits to illegal organisations were discussed within the organisation and carefully watched, before they were invited to join. Finally, someone was assigned to speak to the recruit, someone the recruit already knew, and who belonged to the unit he or she had been assigned to. I heard of only two potential recruits who refused to join, and both promised to keep the secret.

When I was recruited into the Communist Party, it was Hilda Bernstein who first spoke to me. She and Rusty, her husband, were Party stalwarts from the old legal days. He was an architect and a very good political writer, and Hilda had been known as a fine speaker, but had been banned from gatherings for so long that newcomers like me had never heard her speak at a public meeting. Her ban also prevented her going to COD meetings, though she had been a founder member. I had worked with her on the South African Peace Council committee, whose meetings were small enough to masquerade as tea parties of friends. She asked me to stay behind after one of these meetings, which had been held in her house, then told me about the Communist Party, the dangers involved in joining it, and the need for complete secrecy. I was to speak to no one about my membership of the Party, no one at all, except people I worked with in the Party, and who had been introduced to me as Party members.

It was a solemn moment, but I had no hesitation about joining. I was already a convinced socialist; believed – as I still believe – that universal franchise alone isn't enough to correct the terrible inequalities in South Africa, and that radical economic policies are necessary as well. I also knew that, of all political organisations in South Africa, the Communist Party had the best record of resisting racism and apartheid.

Hilda told me I had been assigned to a unit, that the next meeting would be at the flat I then lived in, near the Drill Hall, and that she would bring the other members of the unit with her. So far, she was the only person I knew for certain was a member of the Communist Party, and I had to wait for the meeting to find out more. When the day came, there turned out to be two other members: both women, and both, like Hilda, more than twenty years older than I was; veterans, from the legal days of the Communist Party.

One was Violet Weinberg, whom I already knew as a formidable organising member of the COD. She was married to the photographer, Eli Weinberg, who had been in the trade union movement for many years. He had a splendid singing voice, and had sung in the synagogue choir, as a paid job, for he didn't believe in religion. Neither Violet nor Eli was afraid to bring up their two children, Mark and Sheila, in the way they felt to be right. There is a story about Sheila, at the age of seven, at a demonstration. The police were well acquainted with her parents and, when they took Sheila's name, one of them asked her, "Are you Eli's daughter?" She stood firmly on her rights and replied, "I don't think I have to tell you anything more than my name and address."

The other was Molly Fischer. She and her husband, the advocate Bram Fischer, were from Afrikaner stock, and they were patriotic Afrikaners at that, but they had joined the Communist Party in the legal days, and remained in the Congress movement, though, by that time, they were both banned from its meetings. They lived in a large house with a swimming pool, and comrades were always welcome in that house, to swim in the pool, have tea on the veranda, and later, perhaps a drink.

Molly was a very strong character, in spite of her quiet ways, and great-hearted. She was an indefatigable worker for political prisoners, and thought a lot about their needs. During the school holidays, she sometimes asked me to keep her company on the journey to Pretoria, when she took comforts for them. She was also good at devising ways of doing illegal work, and precautions that should be taken, and she gave that, too, a lot of meticulous thought. She sometimes experimented with disguises, and once appeared at my door in a very simple one – a different kind of hat, tinted glasses – and it was several seconds before I

13

recognised her, which meant the disguise was a success. Once, on their veranda, when Bram asked me a question he should not have asked, according to our rules of security, she intervened: "Bram, don't. What you don't know, you can never let slip by accident."

She had a private reason for grief: her son, the youngest of three children, was seriously and incurably ill, and not likely to live beyond his teens. Also, she felt the misery and the terror of those times very keenly, so, if she sometimes seemed sad and pessimistic, there was more than one cause. I think she took comfort in her garden and in the nearby bird sanctuary, where she took me, on impulse one evening, to watch the birds come in.

"I don't think I've ever seen such a beautiful spring in Johannesburg," I said to her one day late in that terrible year of 1963. Bram was leading the defence in the Rivonia trial, and Molly was working hard on research for the defence case, as well as cooking meals and taking them to the gaol in Pretoria. In reply to my remark, she quoted gloomily, "Look well, for you may not see another." As things turned out, I have seen many springs since, African and European, but that spring was Molly's last. In June 1964, the day after the trial ended, she drowned in the Sand River, north of Bloemfontein, when their car went off the road on the way to Cape Town. I went to her funeral, about a fortnight before I was arrested, and wept. She was a serious loss, as a member and as a friend.

At that first meeting, late in 1960, Hilda, Violet and Molly asked me what code name I wanted to use. They explained that, to protect their identities, all members adopted code names, which were used at meetings, when we referred to each other among ourselves, and when our contact – who was Hilda – reported on us to the area committee. I was a raw recruit, quite overawed, my mind went blank and, unable to think of anything very original, I chose the name Clare, based on my second name, Clarice, my grandmother's name. Someone later started calling me Clara, and the name Clara stuck, till the day of my arrest, and beyond.

From these three experienced, dependable, sometimes overbearing and sometimes aloof women, I learned something of the policies of the Communist Party, and something of how to work underground. Our task in the white area of central Johannesburg was the same task that the COD had tried to carry out: to direct what we had to say to other whites, to urge reason and conscience on them. We discussed our political work and the theory of socialism. We read Communist literature, illegally got from overseas, addressed to a post-office box someone had taken under an assumed name. We distributed leaflets and pamphlets, produced illegally by the Central Committee, leaving them at bus-stops, or sending them through the post, using gloves and disguised handwriting when we addressed the envelopes. We collected names for a clandestine mailing list, and handed them on to Hilda.

We sometimes met in parks and cafes, but felt that made us conspicuous, especially if we had books or sheets of paper in our hands. Most of the time we had to choose to meet in our homes. The danger here was that our homes might be bugged. We dealt with this as best we could, by never speaking aloud key words such as the names of people not present, the name of the Communist Party or the names of any of its structures. When the discussion obliged us to use such words, we mouthed them silently, or wrote them on pieces of paper, which we later burned or put down the lavatory. We used paper too for longer, more complicated statements, and arguments that might reveal what we were doing. Defence lawyers in political trials had learned to use this method of work too, because of the danger of hidden microphones in interview rooms.

After about a year, Molly called in at my flat to tell me that I was being transferred to another unit, and someone from that unit would get in touch with me. She said she, Hilda and Violet were getting another recruit, also a woman; another trainee.

The person who got in touch with me was Pieter Beyleveld, whom I already knew well from my time on the national executive committee of the Congress of Democrats, where he had been national chair. He was a big, quiet man, with a lot of presence. He and the Fischers were the only three white Afrikaners I ever knew of in the Communist Party. He told me once he hadn't learned to speak English till he was twenty-eight years old, and I think it was his experience in the army during World War Two that showed him another side to life.

Bram Fischer was in that unit. He was charming, with a soft voice, but, behind that, there was steel. He was a well-respected person: a president and judge-president of the Free State had been among his forbears; he'd been a Rhodes Scholar, and chairman of the Bar Council. It was generally said he'd have been a judge himself by then, had it not been for his open membership of the Communist Party in the legal days. I suppose we all guessed he was on the Central Committee, but such speculations were quite against our rules, and were never spoken. Within the group, there was a tacit deference to him, as the senior member, and, even when not in the chair, he was merciless about slipshod thinking, inaccuracy in expressing our ideas in debate, careless practice in illegal work.

The rest of us were a good deal younger than Bram and Piet. We were a youth group, and I suppose they were our trainers.

John Benjamin was there; a carpet merchant, and husband of the strong-minded and energetic Pixie, who had worked for the COD before it was banned, and been a mainstay of its regional committee.

There was Ann Nicholson, about twenty-two at that time, small, muscular, energetic, intense in her beliefs and emotions, impulsive in her judgments, quick-tempered. She had been to art school and had developed a variety of talents and skills that were useful to us. After some time in Spain and then in the United Kingdom, she returned to South Africa and worked for the COD for a while, before it was banned. She could not have lived, however economically, on the salary the COD was able to pay her, and she was subsidised by her parents, who sympathised with the aims and policies of the Congresses. Her mother was from a British Communist family and her father, also British, was very proud of his activist daughter.

Lively, attractive, charming, and the youngest of all of us, Ann was a good contact with young people. Our unit, therefore, got the task of organising young people and, chiefly, that meant the "volunteers". She and I were both assigned to this, though I was older than they were, because we had both known them in the COD, and they trusted us. We did the work in consultation with the others in our unit.

The "volunteers" had been organised with rules similar to those in the underground organisations. Group didn't communicate with group, except through the group leaders; members weren't supposed to know who was in the other groups, and they were never to discuss their work except with those in the same group as themselves. It was a strict rule never to use the telephone. Group leaders would visit the scene of an operation beforehand, at the same time of night and on the same night of the week as the operation was planned for, to check on the traffic and numbers of passers-by. We used thieves' slang (gained from novels), and called this "casing the joint". Before the volunteers went out on an operation, everything was settled – exactly what we'd do and where we'd do it, our route, who was to keep watch, and where, at exactly what time, we'd begin, and how long the operation would last.

Every minute increased the chance of our being caught, so we never worked for longer than fifteen minutes, and rarely more than five, and we never worked in one place for longer than three or four minutes. We had to make sure we left no fingerprints on stickers or on the cans of spray paint we threw away down storm-water drains as soon as we had finished with them. We had to put up slogans – and raise flags, as we did on one occasion – between two and three in the morning, when we could usually work without interruption if we worked fast, and when the lights of oncoming cars could be seen a long way off. Small stickers were easier, and could be put up during the course of what looked like a casual evening walk. We no longer carried pots of paint and paste but used spray-paint, bought the previous afternoon, wrapped by the shop assistant and left in its wrapping till, wearing gloves, we unwrapped it.

There were two, and later more, "volunteer" groups in our area. I was in charge of one and, later, in charge of them all. Usually, we organised simultaneous operations, but sometimes a group would go out on its own, after its leader had consulted me about the time. Co-ordination was essential, for the sight of stickers or a painted slogan might alert the police and endanger groups that might happen to be working later the same night.

We did this work because we believed profoundly that it needed to be done. No one else was putting out messages like ours, and it was gratifying to see, in passing, from the window of a bus, something we had put up. Someone once asked me if we enjoyed the activity, found it "fun" or "exciting". I suppose there is often some pleasure in a rush of adrenalin, and there is always pleasure, afterwards, in the feeling of a job well done; but it was tense, nerve-racking, stomach-knotting work.

I dare say it was very slight work, for we weren't blowing up bridges or pylons, or throwing grenades into army camps, but it carried a substantial penalty. If we were caught, there was the certainty of a six-month sentence with a year suspended; Mollie, Pixie, Eve and Mary were proof of that. As time went on, it became increasingly likely that the sentence might be preceded by detention with interrogation, and followed by a banning order. As a group leader and planner, I felt a heavy responsibility for the other members of the group and, before operations, I couldn't sleep. The plans were simple enough – one person deployed as a watcher on this corner, another deployed on that, another painting the slogan – but I mentally rehearsed them, over and over again, for hours, lying in the dark, sometimes till it was time to get up and go out.

The "volunteers" worked well and knew better than to ask what organisation they were working for. All the same, we knew we couldn't expect them to go on for too long, taking orders without taking part in decision-making, and so we worked towards recruiting them into the Party. Soon, most of them had proved their loyalty and their capabilities; we organised political discussion groups for them, and recruited most of them.

Mollie Anderson and Flo Duncan were recruited very early on. Both were in their late twenties, with a lot of character, and serious about the struggle against racism. Flo was a radiographer, had recently moved to Johannesburg from Cape Town, and was fairly new to anti-racist politics. If it hadn't been for her serious feeling for justice and her natural rebelliousness, she might well have spent all her time in a social round, for she was witty and amusing, with a very good figure, dressed more smartly and formally than the rest of us, and liked to go out. She had many friends of both sexes: some who were interested in politics, and many who weren't, and I think she managed to keep the two sides of her life apart.

Mollie Anderson was related to Bram through her mother. However, it wasn't because of the family relationship that she joined. She had come to politics through her own strong sense of right and wrong. She had been born and brought up on a farm in the Free State, had a degree in English from the University of Natal, had worked for the South African Congress of Trade Unions, and later in a bookshop. She was a very controlled, very honest, conscientious person, who took life seriously, and didn't dress up or wear much make-up.

Flo, Mollie and I, in different combinations, carried out a number of operations in the small hours. There was a shop doorway in Pretoria Street in Hillbrow, very near where I lived, where I would stand in the shadows at prearranged times − two, or perhaps two-thirty, in the morning − waiting for Mollie to draw up at the kerb in her small, old car. We'd carry out our task, she would drop me at the door of my block of flats, and we'd both be home in a very short time.

I once met Flo in Edith Cavell Street at two in the morning, and we walked over the hill, through back streets, to Clarendon Place. We both wore black trousers and sweaters, in the hope of being inconspicuous in the dark, for, in those days, that part of Hillbrow was dark, silent and deserted at that time of night. So great was the trust the "volunteers" had in each other that, when Flo and I arrived in Clarendon Place, we knew that the third person, Paul Trewhela, would, at that moment, be taking up his prearranged place at the top of the hill overlooking Louis Botha Avenue. We had synchronised our watches the previous afternoon, and agreed that Paul would watch both ways for the lights of oncoming cars, cough if it was necessary to warn us and, after exactly three minutes, would make his way back to his flat. Flo watched the side streets, I sprayed a huge slogan on the wall of a block of flats, and threw the canister down a drain. In three minutes it was over, and Flo and I were back in a dark side street, walking home.

After that, Paul insisted that he wanted to paint the slogan when the three of us worked together. I think he felt slogan-painting, as a dangerous job, was suitable for men, and that he was only half a man if he stood by while a woman did it. After some thought, I gave in to him, to spare his pride. It didn't prove disastrous, but it wasn't the most efficient way of working either, for my blackboard experience and my poor eyesight made me a better slogan-painter than a watcher.

Paul was a bright young journalist on a Johannesburg newspaper. He was also producing a small cyclostyled journal for MK, but the rest of us didn't know that at the time, and, if those who knew him suspected it, we said nothing. It was he who supplied the slogan, "Apartheid is the killer", which we used often. He was soon recruited into the youth group, and he, Flo and I did more than one operation together, for we lived within a short walking distance of each other, and therefore didn't have to use a car, which might have made us more conspicuous.

Paul used to take his younger sister, Beverley, with him as his partner on some "volunteer" operations. She came to one or two discussion evenings, but hadn't yet been recruited by the time we were arrested. After some time though, their working partnership came to an abrupt end, because of a circumstance none of us had foreseen. One night at about nine, they were putting up stickers, strolling through the neighbourhood where Beverley still lived with their parents, when they saw someone approaching. Paul knew the traditional drill: if you don't want people to think you're doing something illegal, pretend to be lovers. He acted quickly, and clasped his sister passionately in his arms. When the person drew nearer, he turned out to be a friend of their parents. He recognised them both, and greeted them. After that, neither Paul nor Beverley felt inclined to do that kind of work together again.

There was a young doctor, newly qualified, Constantinos Gazides, known as Costa. Perhaps his view of politics was sometimes romantic, but he was sincere, enthusiastic, sometimes rash, always brave. He was one of our most able slogan-painters and poster-stickers, and he and I had first worked together just before the State of Emergency in 1960 (a time we later thought of as the easy days) putting up very large posters, with flour-and-water paste, at five in the morning.

We worked together again, a few years later. Illegal ANC flags were put up in all areas in the Johannesburg district, to greet the dawn of Freedom Day, June 26th, the day the Freedom Charter had been adopted at the Congress of the People in Kliptown in 1956. I later heard that, in some of the black townships, the flags were paper pennants stuck over pieces of waste ground. Costa and I had the task of hoisting a full-sized, black, green and gold flag in central Johannesburg.

Costa "cased" a hotel near the station, that had a flagpole on the roof. I didn't know how to hoist a flag, but he did. My role was to keep watch while he worked, and to get us both down behind a skylight if a night watchman, or anyone else, came along. We booked into the hotel as Mr and Mrs, at about ten in the evening, and paid for the room, saying that we were travelling and would be leaving very early. In the room, Costa produced a pack of cards, and we sat on the bed playing cards till two in the morning, when Costa led the way to the roof, and put the flag up. We left at once after that, for it was better to get out of the place before our work was discovered, and I wanted a few hours' sleep in my own bed, only a few hundred yards away, before facing a full day's teaching.

Costa did a year's housemanship in Durban, and joined the Party youth group on his return, but came to only one meeting. He got married, and felt obliged to retire from activities, since everything we were doing was a strict secret, and he didn't know how he'd explain whole evenings away from home, and occasional absences from the matrimonial bed in the middle of the night.

Our last recruit on this list was our mistake: Gerard (or Gerald) Ludi, who was a police spy. He was a shifty-eyed person, who seemed oddly ignorant of our aims and ways of thought; but he was on friendly terms with a range of Party members, young and old, who all recommended him. I hardly knew him, and the only argument I had against his recruitment was a gut feeling, which I didn't put forward as an argument, because I felt it was no argument at all. It was a lesson to me to put more trust in my gut feelings in the future.

Once recruited, Ludi was eager for information but, at the same time, it was difficult to get him to take part in any activity. He was leader of a "volunteer" group and, in conference with me, he always had an excuse to prevent its going out on any operation. I doubt whether he ever took it out at all. This was particularly frustrating for Ann, at the time when she was in this group, and she eventually approached me in real anger, to ask me why I was stifling "volunteer" activity in the area. Ludi had lied to her; he had told her that, in my capacity as leader of all the groups, I had refused to allow it. We discovered his duplicity too late to save ourselves from the damage he was doing us by passing on information to the police.

Another group of "volunteers" consisted of young and enthusiastic men, friends of Ann: Terry Bell, his younger brother Michael, and one or two others. Terry and the Boys, which was how we generally referred

to them, were the most daring and inventive of all the "volunteers". I
went out on an operation with them once, at the beginning, to teach
them our rules of security and, after that, I left them to it, with the
proviso that they should check with me when planning the time of any
operation. After that, if we saw "Apartheid is the killer", or some such
slogan, written in some spectacular place in our area, like the side of a
railway bridge or of a mine dump, we knew it was the work of Terry
and the Boys.

We were grooming them for membership of the Party, but they
hadn't been in the COD, and we thought they needed more knowledge
of political theory first. I managed to set up one or two meetings for
them with ANC members and trade unionists, but they hadn't been
recruited by the time we were arrested. Like Beverley, they had a lucky
escape but, at the time, they didn't see it like that, and I was sorry to
hear, years later, that they had been deeply offended at not having been
asked to join.

They were sincerely eager to help. Terry and one of the others came
to see me late one night, when I had put out my light and was preparing
for sleep. They sat in the dark, on the end of my bed, and told me
they'd heard from people they knew that there were to be more arrests.
They had contacts, drinking companions, among the police. I told them
I'd pass the information on, and, the next day, after school, I caught a
bus to pass the warning on to Bram. "Who's going to be arrested?" he
demanded angrily. "When? What are we supposed to do?" I was
surprised by his irritable response, but later I understood it. No one
could prepare for a warning like that. It did no more than create
anxiety, and Bram was deeply anxious already.

During this time came the shock and disruption of the arrests at
Rivonia. We weren't affected directly, for none of the "volunteers" or
the young people in the units had been there, and most of them didn't
know such a place existed. I had only an inkling, because of the efforts
I'd had to make, through intermediaries, to get silk-screen equipment
for Ann to make posters. Once existence of the place was revealed, we
understood well that no one should have known about it except those
who needed to go there for some sound reason. Ludi, the most recent
newcomer, was the exception, and thought differently. He was angry
and indignant that we hadn't been told, and spoke as if he thought we
had been deprived of our rights by not being informed. We were
patient with what we thought was his ignorance. With hindsight, I
realise he was disappointed not to have been able to present the
information to the police as the first coup of his career as a spy.

There was a reshuffle. Beyleveld had to shed his work in the unit. He was still on the area committee, but now as contact with the Johannesburg District Committee. He had been moved on to a reconstituted Central Committee too, but we weren't told that at the time. He co-ordinated "volunteer" activities throughout the district and, each time an operation was planned in my area, I had to visit him in his office to check that the date and the time were safe. I think he must have been in touch with MK operations too, otherwise our precautions wouldn't have been effective; but it was against all our rules of security to ask him about this.

I continued to work with Beyleveld, on another level too; I was moved on to the area committee, taking his place as contact with the youth group. We split this group into two, because it was growing large, and our rule was for very small units. Flo and Mollie formed the second unit, and I was contact for that as well. It wasn't good security, but we had to balance one security risk against another, and decided not to enlarge the area committee any further. Pixie, who had recently been released from prison, was organised in this unit, but she and John dropped out of activity soon after that.

The next year of my life was very busy: area meetings, regular meetings with two different units; "volunteer" work, which, on its own, took a lot of organising. All arrangements had to be made face-to-face, because we didn't use the telephone. My teaching involved a lot of marking, I rarely had enough sleep, and my teaching suffered. A sixteen-year-old girl said to me once, very frankly, "You're so crabby these days", and I had no reply, no defence, because I knew what she said was true.

On the area committee, I learned more about the higher structures of Party organisation. Like our area units, the committee was white. Representatives from African, Indian, coloured and white areas met only at the District and Central Committees, and these meetings had to be set up very carefully. At the time I am writing about, women were very rarely, if ever, part of these structures. The men who comprised the higher, mixed-race committees believed that the presence of women was a danger for, should the police raid the meeting, they might manufacture evidence for charges under the Immorality Act, which forbade sexual relations between people of different races. At the time, there seemed to be sense in the argument. Women remained in the lower, racially based groups. It's undeniable that the organisation was dominated by men.

The people on the area committee were all contacts with groups, or with individuals, who, for reasons of safety, hadn't been grouped, but communicated one-to-one with their contacts.

Hilda Bernstein was there, still as contact with Molly, Violet and the fourth woman. After the arrests at Rivonia, where her husband, Rusty, had been among those taken, she suggested that the area committee insulate itself with new code names. That meeting at which she made the suggestion was being held in some haste, because of the security risks, and our minds went blank, but Hilda kept her head and, after the fashion of eeny-meeny-miny-mo, she went round the circle, allocating names of current brands of instant coffee. I got the name of Kenna, which I used thereafter on the area committee, though in the units I still used the name Clara.

Esther Barsel was an important figure on that committee. She was a commercial traveller, a married woman with three young daughters, small, strong-willed, hard-working, and good at underground organising. To keep her as inconspicuous as possible, the Party had pulled her out of the COD some time before it was banned, for she was contact with a number of secret or nearly-secret Party members.

These included a highly secret group called the "D" group, which used typewriters and duplicating machines, and kept them in a safe house. The lists of names and addresses our units compiled for the mailing list were passed on to them by Esther; and then they were supposed to copy them out, and destroy the original pieces of paper, which could be traced back to members.

Esther reported regularly on the progress and morale of this unit, but gave few details on what it was doing, for not all the work it did was for the area. It was doing Central Committee and MK work as well, which made it a nodal point between MK and the Party: sensitive, and even dangerous. On the area committee, though we might guess this, we were never told it, still working on the principle that no one should know more than was necessary. We used the code names when reporting on our groups, and it was a safeguard, for we couldn't give away what we didn't know. Of course, when Hilda reported, I knew two of the names she mentioned, though I didn't know the third, but I knew nothing at all about who was in the "D" group, nor much about what they were doing until, when we were on trial ourselves, I read about their trial in the papers. I don't think I'd ever heard the names of John Matthews or David Kitson until they were arrested and detained, shortly before we were, given away by someone who had made a statement to the police. I did know the name of another member: Lionel Gay, whom I had met once, and who broke under interrogation and, at their trial, gave evidence against them.

None of us had any objection to links with MK; we assumed that they existed. None of us questioned the need for armed struggle, for at that time it seemed one of the few effective ways left to us of opposing the government. Piet, however, was always at pains to emphasise that MK and the Communist Party were separate organisations. This was for security reasons, because anything done in the name of MK was classed as sabotage, and the penalties were much more severe than those for the kind of work we were doing. "Don't *say* that!" I once heard him shout, when a young comrade – I think it was Ann – loyally identified with what MK was doing, and referred to it as "we".

Esther was also in contact – in the Party sense, as well as the personal – with her husband, Hymie, a staunch, good-natured man. For years he had carried out the thankless task of running the Friends of the Soviet Union, which had had a large following during World War Two, but had lost support since the beginning of the Cold War. She was also in touch with her friends, Ann and Issy Heymann. It was a good way of organising for, if people were known to be friends, it attracted little attention when they met. Like the Weinbergs and the Fischers, the Barsels and the Heymanns had a long history of activity in the Communist Party in the old legal days, and in the trade union movement.

There were two more veterans from the days when the Communist Party had been legal. One was Lewis Baker, unassuming, likeable, with a dry, self-deprecating sense of humour. He had been born in Benoni, a small Reef town near Johannesburg. Many consider it a one-horse place, but he had never left it. He had studied law in Johannesburg, travelling in and out each day, and had then set up as an attorney back home in Benoni. He kept in touch with one or two members in his neighbourhood, whom I didn't know.

Another was Norman Levy, teacher of history, to whom I tried to telephone the news, on the morning I was arrested. He had been in the Treason Trial of 1956, and had been one of those released after a year. He was contact with a unit which included Philippa, his wife at that time, and which was joined later by Sylvia Neame, a member transferred from Cape Town, who had come to do an honours course at Witwatersrand University. She had started off in the youth group, which meant she too was known to Ludi.

There was a mysterious figure, who didn't seem to represent any group, and who, for a long time, I knew only by his code name. His real name was Viv Ezra, and I learned it only when I saw his photograph in the paper. He had disappeared suddenly and reappeared in London, and not a moment too soon. His name had been mentioned in the Rivonia trial, as the person who had bought Liliesleaf Farm, Rivonia, which meant he had been consciously acting as an agent of the underground liberation movement.

I remember very clearly some Party operations I took part in.

One incident is an illustration of the difficulty older comrades sometimes had in adapting to clandestine methods. The Party planned a nationwide leaflet distribution, and I was given the task of taking a consignment of leaflets from Johannesburg to Durban. Soon after dark one Thursday evening, I caught the bus to Michael Harmel's house. Like Bram, he had been a well-known Communist for many years, since before the Party was banned. He took me in his car to fetch the leaflets, stopped outside a house, went in alone, and came out with a very large, very heavy suitcase, locked, so that if I was arrested while carrying it, I could plead in court that I didn't know what was in it.

I knew the house. It belonged to Ralph and Minnie Sepel, whom I knew as close acquaintances, as friends of friends. They weren't in the area structures, and I'd never have guessed that they were active in the underground at all, had Beyleveld not previously asked me not to visit them. He had given no explanation, but the only possible reason could have been a fear that, if I were followed by the police, I might lay a trail to them. Now, I had discovered something further, that I should never have known: that they were working for structures other than the area structures, and were storing illegal literature.

Michael dropped me off at my flat, and I kept the suitcase there until the next day, after school, when, according to instructions, I took it with me on the overnight train to Durban. I tried to look like a lady travelling, rather than an activist transporting leaflets, and wore a sleek dress, with stiletto heels, which made carrying that weight along railway platforms even more painful. The next morning, I put the suitcase in the left luggage at Durban station, and visited my mother for a few hours, hoping it would keep my nerves calm. It didn't. At two o'clock in the afternoon, I had to meet someone – I hadn't been told whom – in the town gardens in front of the City Hall.

The gardens lie between three of Durban's busiest streets, and are overlooked by the Royal Hotel, which, in those days, had a wide veranda in front, where people (whites only, of course) sat and sipped their drinks. I felt conspicuous carrying this enormous piece of baggage into the gardens, and was surprised when the person who arrived to take it was MP Naicker, generally known as MP, a very well-known political leader in Natal.

I think he took a rash chance, for he was the kind of person the police used to follow, and there was every likelihood that he might have been followed then. And, if there were any interested onlookers, I wonder what they might have made of it. They might have thought that I was a white woman waiting for an Indian driver to pick up her suitcase; but why should I wait in the town gardens, instead of on the pavement? And why didn't MP bring his car to the pavement beside the gardens, instead of disappearing, with the case, down one of the lanes leading to the Esplanade? The handover went off safely, but it was the kind of action that might easily have drawn attention to us, and given the police a bridge between legal and illegal political activities.

Other operations were better organised. Once, when Nelson Mandela was in hiding, my flat was used for an afternoon meeting between him and Winnie and their children. I was told he would arrive first. He arrived dead on time and, even then, when I answered the door to a very tall man in a dust coat, chauffeur's cap and dark glasses, I hesitated a moment, not recognising him. His family arrived a minute or two later, and I went out for the afternoon. The place was empty when I got back at half-past six, as arranged.

Someone once gave me a ticket for a parcel that was waiting at the OK Bazaars left parcels counter. It had come from the "D" group, and contained two lots of leaflets, envelopes and stamps. I dropped one lot off with the youth unit, and then sat with Flo and Mollie while we laboriously addressed the envelopes with our left hands (it was supposed to disguise handwriting), stamped them, put in the leaflets, and left separately, each with a bundle to put in the post, wearing gloves all the time. The work was all done in one long evening, because it was safer to get rid of such material as soon as possible.

There was sometimes a lighter side. Once, Ann and I bought a children's toy printing set and a packet or two of adhesive labels, to make stickers. Wearing gloves, we printed them with slogans, late one afternoon, in my flat. We went out in the early evening, got rid of the equipment in a nearby dustbin, and then put up the stickers in hallways and lifts. Everything went off smoothly, for we were both experienced operators by that time, but we realised too late that we should have bought a separate inking pad, one intended for adults. The ink in the toy set was thoughtfully designed to wash out of clothes, and the wet sponges we used (in those days, adhesive labels all had to be moistened) smeared the stickers as we put them up, and washed some of them quite clean.

It was a very small group of whites "on the left" in Johannesburg, as in all the other towns in South Africa. Nearly everyone knew nearly everyone else, and it was no secret that most of us had been in the COD. In one way it made things easier, for it was natural that people like Ann, Mollie, Flo, Paul, Costa and I should visit each other, or have coffee together in Hillbrow and, as in the case of the Barsels and the Heymanns, it was possible to organise meetings without attracting too much attention.

Some of us – those with families – lived in houses, mostly in Yeoville, Bellevue or Orange Grove, and most of the single people lived in flats in Hillbrow. There was a low-rent, three-bedroomed, shabby but pleasant cottage in a back yard in Orange Grove, which served as a kind of commune, shared by Flo, Ann, Sylvia, Mark Weinberg, me and others, in different combinations, at different times. There was no electrically heated water there so, in the last year before our arrest, when Sylvia Neame was sharing the place with Mark Weinberg, and I was living in Hillbrow, she formed the habit of visiting me quite often, late in the afternoon, to have a bath. She had a key, in case she arrived before I did. When she was out of the bath, we'd have a drink and talk.

These were enjoyable social occasions, which we both needed. Sylvia, inclined by nature to be withdrawn and anxious, vehement in her opinions and feelings, was hard hit in that last year. She had serious, private causes for anxiety. In addition, she'd been arrested and detained for a couple of months, and then placed under a banning order. This interrupted her studies, and caused her further anxiety over whether she might lose her scholarship. She hadn't been in Johannesburg long, and detention and banning circumscribed her life, making it difficult, if not impossible, for her to meet new people and form new friendships. As one of the few people in our social circle still left unbanned, I was one of the few she could visit freely.

I, for my part, was so stretched that I saw very few people, except at work or at meetings. Sylvia's visits were welcome. So were Flo's when she lived near me in Hillbrow. Her sense of humour and ready, slightly acid, tongue always made me feel more cheerful. We laughed and joked, and it was a relief from the strain of our lives.

These were easy relationships, for we were united by a feeling of urgency and danger, and didn't have to deceive each other. Of course, certain subjects were taboo: for instance Sylvia and I both knew we couldn't ask each other about the activities of our respective units but, apart from that, our talk was frank, because we knew where we stood.

Where other relationships were concerned, underground work had the effect of imposing a sad isolation.

I had made good friends among the staff during my five years at the private high school. Their loyalty, generosity and humour were to be a source of strength to me later, but I couldn't be perfectly open with them. I don't find friendship possible without honest exchange of feelings and opinions and, of course, I spoke frankly to them about my attitude to government policies, to race discrimination and to the ANC. They shared these attitudes, more or less. When I look back, it strikes me that more than half of them were unconventional South African whites because they weren't South African born. Lucy Klug had been born in Lodz in Poland in the 1920s, and her family had come to South Africa as Jewish refugees. Elena Thomas, born in Rome, and Dinah Berry, born in Jerusalem, had both come to South Africa as war brides at the end of World War Two.

I couldn't be frank about my membership of illegal organisations and what I did in the evenings, and they never could understand why I was hardly ever free for, after the COD was banned, there seemed no reason for my being so busy. Lucy's theory was that it was against my principles to attend racially segregated cinemas and theatres, and nothing would convince her this wasn't so. Eventually, Elena came to understand too well. She had some understanding of the situation political activists were in because her husband, Jimmy, an industrial council secretary, had loyally continued to employ Helen Joseph and others through gathering troubles. She said to me bluntly: "You're a member of another organisation, not only the Congress of Democrats," and I had to reply, "What are you talking about? I don't know what you mean." Dinah knew better than to ask such questions, and so did Wolfie Noriskin, whose niece's husband was an activist in Cape Town and had been detained during the 1960 State of Emergency.

New acquaintances stopped inviting me anywhere, offended by repeated excuses. There was a young drama teacher at the private college, who tried hard to make friends with me. I liked her very much, but didn't know how to engage in frank, relaxed chatter with her, for, by that time, there seemed to be little or nothing of my life after hours that wasn't taboo. She must have found me strangely cold and unforthcoming. Making friends with women and men outside our circle was difficult; for there were too many unexplained engagements in my life, too many activities in my small flat that strangers shouldn't see.

I neglected old, close friendships too. Once Margery, a dear friend, telephoned to ask me to come and see her at her home in Parkview, and I replied, "I can't, I'm busy." Her voice was full of indignation and hurt feelings when she said: "Jean, we've been friends for years, and now I'm going overseas. We may not meet again for a long time. Surely you can come out and see me." I felt very sad and very ashamed, but I couldn't go to Parkview on the evening she wanted me to, nor any other evening that week; nor could I give her the real, pressing explanation: that there would be people waiting for me, and I had no way of letting them know I wasn't coming. In illegal work, it was out of the question to keep people waiting, unless one had been arrested.

For me, that work and that life came to an end, and a very different life began, when I arrived at Pretoria Central Prison, Female Section, penned in the back of a two-door car, with two security policemen in the front. It was Friday, July 3rd 1964, and I wasn't to walk free again until Thursday, April 11th 1968.

CHAPTER 4

Detention

I was received into the gaol by the chief wardress, known as a "matron", who wore a sergeant's stripes on her khaki uniform. She opened my jars of creams and lotions, one by one, and my lipsticks, to examine them, and ran her finger and thumb along the seams of all my clothes.

I was surprised at her manners when she exclaimed loudly at the sight of a pair of knickers, and held them up to show them to a middle-aged man who stood silently next to her. "God!" she said to him in Afrikaans, "They're red!" They were, indeed, red, but I didn't see what business that was of hers, or of his. I had more urgent things to worry about than whether this man saw my red knickers or not, but I was angry with her because it was clear she'd intended to humiliate me. With more experience of prison, I was to discover that it's the habit of prison authorities to behave in an unmannerly way to prisoners, as part of the process of breaking them down.

The man's expression didn't change. I learned over the years that it never did. He wasn't introduced to me then, but I was to get to know him as Colonel (later Brigadier) Aucamp, liaison between the prisons and the security police. No doubt, the matron had hoped to amuse him, and so gain his favour. The security police were very powerful.

By the time I was escorted upstairs by a wardress, they had stripped me of some of my possessions, and locked them in a cupboard. These included stockings and suspender belt, in case I used them to hang myself; cigarettes and matches, which were supposed to be a fire hazard; handbag mirror, which I might use for cutting my wrists; eyebrow tweezers, which might be used as a lock-picking tool; nail file, nail scissors and needle, which might be used as dangerous weapons; wristwatch, which might help me co-ordinate a plan of escape with friends outside; and money, which I might use to bribe my way out. I had nothing to read, or to write with either, for such consolations were forbidden under the regulations governing ninety-day detention.

It was the first time I'd seen a cell door, with spy-hole and outer grille. The keys hung from a long leather strap wound round the wardress's waist, and were bigger than any keys I'd ever imagined. The cell was unexpectedly large and pleasant, and overlooked the prison grounds. It didn't dawn on me till later that this was a condemned cell, and that an inner window, that gave on to the landing, was the one through which a watch is kept during the condemned prisoner's last days.

I was alone with those clothes and other possessions that hadn't been confiscated, an iron bedstead with a flock mattress, a cupboard with shelves, a small rectangular wooden stool, and a sanitary bucket. There was a wicker chair too, something I never saw in any other cell. I don't know whether it was meant as a privilege for the condemned, or as a comfort for the wardress who sat with her.

The time was about 11.30 a.m., and a metal dish of food was waiting on top of the cupboard. It was already cold and, even when warm, it couldn't have been very inviting, but it was my midday meal, the main meal of the day. This was my first encounter with prison life and prison hours. Supper, such as it was, would come at about five and, after that, it was a long haul till breakfast the next morning.

I had some idea of how difficult it was going to be. We had all heard of the physical torture. I knew something, too, of what psychological effects to expect as a result of solitary confinement, for Kurt Danziger, then professor of psychology at Cape Town University, had done work on the experiences of detainees and, staying in his house on holiday in Cape Town that year, in January, I'd discussed it with him a good deal. He'd given me some articles he'd written; I'd handed them over to the area committee when I got back to Johannesburg, and we'd discussed them in my units. I had seen how difficult Sylvia had found it to talk about her experiences after her first detention, and how many of her reactions since then had seemed paranoid. It seemed to me that the sooner I began trying to adjust to this situation, the easier it would be, and so the first thing I did was to put my clothes and other possesssions away on the shelves.

It didn't take long, because I hadn't brought much, only what I thought I would need in detention: two changes of casual everyday clothing, my winter coat, a good grey flannel dress with high-heeled shoes in case I had to appear in court, washing bag and cosmetics, a warm, easily washable nightdress and the warm dressing gown I'd been wearing while the police searched my flat. It reached to the floor and buttoned up to my chin, and I was thankful for the instinct that had made me buy it, only a week or two before, for there was no heating in the cells.

I changed into trousers and a sweater, had a few mouthfuls of the food, and then fell asleep under a grey prison blanket. It had been a long, tiring morning.

I couldn't have slept more than half an hour or so because, when I awoke, the wardresses had gone off for lunch. I heard shrill cries from down the corridor, distorted by echoes and, after a while, recognised familiar voices calling my name. Ann, Esther, Flo, Pixie and Sylvia were there, Beverley too, and Sheila Weinberg, now aged eighteen. They had recognised the sound of my smoker's cough. They said they were in very small cells, with black walls, and some without windows, partitioned off a huge hall, and with ceilings of chicken-wire. They were amazed and envious when I told them that I had a cell with green walls and a view. I told them I believed that Norman had been arrested; I heard that Pixie's husband, John, was still free, so their children were cared for. Hymie had been picked up at the same time as Esther, and the girls, aged sixteen, eleven and eight, had been getting ready for school when it happened.

That was all the news we succeeded in exchanging, that first day. The others could speak to each other easily, but the acoustics of the place created difficulties between them and me. It seemed that sound carried clearly only from Esther's cell to mine, so she had to climb on to her cupboard and call over the partition, to relay messages from the others, and to relay my messages back; difficult for her, as she was physically the smallest of us all, apart from Ann. I had to climb on to the cupboard under my internal window, to hear her and reply. That meant a lot of climbing, a lot of loud shouting, and a lot of repetition, and it could be done only at midday and in the evenings, when the wardresses were off duty. Communication had to be confined to essentials.

Through that inner window, I could see and hear something of the wardresses and other prisoners coming and going, and so I became aware almost at once of the atmosphere of prison: the silence, the pervading sense of sadness and gloom. I cannot describe it adequately. Films never quite capture it. Outside my cell, black prisoners in tent-like uniforms, heads wrapped in cloths, whispered to each other as they cleaned and polished the stairs and the landing. The quiet was broken only by the wardresses screaming orders. It seemed that screaming and shouting were thought the correct way to speak to prisoners. The voices reverberated in those large, empty spaces enclosed by brick and concrete.

During the following few days, I found out that whistling wasn't allowed, nor singing, except on Sundays, and then only hymns. On the two Sundays I was there, I heard the sound of singing from the cells downstairs, and I can never forget those hymns sung in Pretoria Central, so slow, so drear, so lacking in spirit. *Nearer, My God, to Thee* was often sung and, even now, the tune vividly brings those days back to me.

Never before, certainly not in any school where I'd taught, had I experienced such emphasis on such petty rules. We learned them, one by one, as wardresses shouted orders at us. At seven every morning, the matron in charge went from cell to cell with a wardress, who wheeled a trolley carrying porridge, bread and a warmish liquid they called coffee. While this was going on, prisoners were required to stand to attention beside their neatly made beds, fully dressed, their hands behind their backs. I overslept one morning, and was still in bed when breakfast came. The matron was very angry. "This is the last time," she screamed, "the last time I want to find you in bed." I was sure she had no power to enforce prison rules on me, because detainees were prisoners of the security branch, and not subject to prison regulations, so I replied, just as rudely, "What will you do? Lock me in gaol?" After that, though, I was always ready when she came. I felt at a disadvantage, looking up at her from among the bedclothes.

The ablution block for white prisoners was in the courtyard, near the matron's office. Neither bathrooms nor lavatories had doors. We were all taken there each morning, for the regulation bath and "exercise" hour. After we came out of the bathroom, we spent the rest of the hour in the courtyard, where there was some greenery. Wardresses kept us apart, and stopped us talking to each other, and we sat around wretchedly on the grass, exchanging glances, trying to enjoy the winter sunshine, and smoking our cigarettes, which we were allowed to have during this time. Small physical comforts, like cigarettes, are very important to prisoners, and nearly all of us were smokers, then. There were many more smokers in those days than there are now.

We all complained about boredom except Esther, who said she was sleeping day and night. She said this was because, after months of stress and meetings, she was now relieved of all responsibility, and no one could expect her to do anything.

The security police allowed her a visit to discuss family business. It was from Hymie's sister and brother-in-law, who had moved into the house with the children. Through another visitor – Beverley's, I think – we heard that we had been part of the first of two waves of mass arrests, all over the country, and that, among others, Paul, Costa, and Piet Beyleveld had been taken. I knew that, a week or two before, Piet had had word that his name was being mentioned in statements made to the police by prisoners in detention, and was very anxious about it.

On the second day, we agreed on a united demand for Bibles, which we knew were being issued to ninety-day detainees. The prisoner's right to a Bible was deemed to override other rules, though – as I have learned since – getting hold of religious writings was often difficult for black prisoners and for followers of religions other than Christianity. Within a day or two, we got Bibles from the prison stock. I'd read as far as the Book of Kings, by the time I was moved, and was struggling through the tedious part about the dimensions of the Temple. I realise now that it seemed longer and more difficult than it really is, because solitary confinement was beginning to take its toll. Kurt Danziger's tests had shown that concentration, and even reasoning, were rapidly affected.

Within the first few days, we were all subjected to a token interrogation, and we all replied that we had nothing to say. I had a second interrogation, a day or two later, when I was taken, with a wardress in attendance, to Compol Buildings, police headquarters, in the centre of Pretoria. The building had an imposing entrance, and a number of small, dusty, comfortless offices at the back. The experience was alarming. They threatened me with charges, and I'm glad I had the presence of mind to reply that, if I was to be charged, I wanted to consult a lawyer. No legal consultations were allowed in ninety-day detention; they had tried a bluff, and I had called it. They kept me waiting for two very anxious hours on a wooden bench in the corridor – I didn't have my watch, but heard a city clock strike – and then took me into an office to ask me if I wanted to make a statement. I replied that I didn't, so was taken back to the gaol, and to my plate of congealed dinner some wardress had left on the cupboard.

Because we weren't convicted prisoners, food from outside was allowed, though the packages were searched. Comrades and sympathisers outside were working hard in an effort to get a token, at least, to each of the hundreds of people in detention at that time. They didn't have the resources to send in food every day, and it came in only on Sundays. There was never much – a hard-boiled egg, a sweet or two, perhaps a small packet of peanuts, or a few biscuits – but the benefit to our morale was beyond measuring, for each little box was labelled with a name, and was a sign that families and friends knew where we were.

Through the outer window one afternoon, I saw Dinah, my teacher friend, step out of her small car. She had had some experience of the struggle against British rule in Palestine, and so didn't suffer from the bewilderment many whites felt at the prospect of visiting prisoners. Elegant and graceful as always, she walked across the open ground, with a charming, expectant expression on her face, as if she were arriving at a party, and with a carrier bag hanging from one hand. It was a wonderful surprise to see her. I whistled to get her attention, and waved. She looked up, and must have seen me behind the grille, because she waved back.

A watching warder reported the episode. I was taken from my cell and, when I was returned to it, I found the window had been boarded up. I demanded to see the commanding officer of the prison and, rather to my surprise, was taken to him at once. I argued that this must be against health regulations since, now that nothing was open besides the window on to the landing, there was no cross-ventilation in my cell. "There's the door," he replied. "How often is the door open in gaol?" I asked angrily. It seemed he accepted my argument, because the boards were taken down again, within a few minutes. There had been an interesting break in the monotony of the day, and I had learned that waving through windows isn't permitted in gaol.

Dinah's bag of comforts was brought in to me: another diversion. I'd never eaten halva before, but I have loved it ever since. I ate the whole slab, and a whole packet of biscuits as well, and sent the rest out to be kept with my other things, in time for the hunger strike we had agreed would begin the next day. We intended it as a protest against the injustice of imprisonment without trial, and as part of a demand that we be either charged or released.

In the morning, when our breakfast arrived, we refused it, and asked for it to be taken away. After going away to confer briefly, the matron and wardresses returned to tell us that the food would be left in our cells, and it was up to us whether we ate it or not. It wasn't difficult to abstain from it, since it wasn't very palatable – that is, except for the bread. We used to wonder who the baker at Pretoria Central was, because the bread there was the best rough wholewheat any of us had ever tasted, and it was freshly baked every morning.

It was agreed between us that those with stomach ulcers – Flo, Sylvia and I – might stop, after a token fast, when we felt we couldn't go on. I lasted for only two days. We all lost weight quickly while we were fasting and, from one morning to the next, we could see changes in each other. Beverley and Sheila in particular, plump young women at the beginning, seemed to shrink to half their previous size, and their trousers began to hang shapelessly.

Before this, I had often wondered about the value of hunger strikes, because they seemed to me to be more harmful to the hunger strikers than to their captors. I learned a lesson. As evidence of united action, our hunger strike clearly alarmed those in authority for, the day we began it, the commanding officer of the prison had us brought to the office in turn, and urged each of us to persuade the others to eat. We refused to do any such thing.

The danger of adverse publicity, our solid loyalty to each other, and the fact that we had all refused to make statements, must have been why they separated us so quickly. By the time we had been in detention a fortnight, we were dispersed in gaols and police stations along the Reef and in Pretoria, and only Flo was left in that dark, echoing hall, where she spent six weeks alone.

I was the first to go. Eleven days after our arrest, I was moved without warning. When a wardress called me away from morning "exercise", I thought I was being taken to another interrogation, and waved hastily to the others before I was led indoors to my cell. That was the last I saw of them for six weeks, for I was told to pack my things and, within ten minutes, I was off, in the back of a two-door Beetle, with no goodbyes.

I wasn't told where I was being taken and, when we arrived, I wasn't told the name of the place, nor where it was. This kind of thing was done deliberately, to create a feeling of intense insecurity in the prisoner. It's frightening enough to feel that one's life and surroundings are completely controlled by the whims and arbitrary actions of others. It's worse when those others are patently hostile.

That afternoon, alone in my new cell, I felt acutely anxious, terrified, panic-stricken, almost beyond control. That, in itself, was cause for further fear, for I was afraid of what I might do in a state of such emotional disintegration. From the beginning, the police had revealed that they knew I knew about a sector of our underground organisation. They had called me Clara, and wanted me to tell them more. I dreaded going to pieces and making a statement.

I was saved, that afternoon, by patience: not the virtue, but the card game, which I have used as stress relief ever since I wrote university examinations. Among what remained of Dinah's gift of food, which had been brought with me, was a round box of processed cheese. I tore the strips of cardboard into fifty-two tiny pieces, and marked them with lipstick and a ballpoint refill which the policewoman who had searched me had left in my pocket. The idea was Sylvia's; I remembered her telling me she'd done it in her first detention. The activity took my mind off my troubles, so did the games of patience that followed and, by the end of the afternoon, I felt much better.

I felt worried and depressed the following Sunday, when no little parcel arrived for me, because it meant people outside didn't know where I was. Strangely though, a visit from two detectives, two days before, had made me feel quite strong. The interrogation was short and to the point. They told me more of what they already knew, and urged me to make a statement. They threatened me with prolonged detention, and reminded me that Alfred Nzo had been in detention for two hundred and eighty-seven days. Then they left. It was a sobering occasion, especially the mention of Alfred Nzo's experience, for the mere fourteen days I'd been in a solitary cell – less than one-twentieth of two hundred and eighty-seven – seemed like a very long time. In spite of this though, I went back to my cell with more confidence for, facing the security police, I knew there was no question of my giving them information, not unless interrogations got much tougher than that. I didn't know how I'd behave under torture. That was something I had to think about.

The nature of the information the police had made its source quite clear. It was from Gerald Ludi. I was deeply disturbed to find how much they knew, but took some comfort in the fact that Ludi had gone no further than a small "volunteer" group and a small Communist Party unit, and that, in all, he knew only about half a dozen people. In both these groups, he had known me as contact person with other organisational structures, which meant that the police would naturally see me as a lead, and put pressure on me. That wasn't a pleasant thought. I felt, in a small way, like Horatius holding the bridge, or the Dutch boy in the story, stopping a leak in the dyke.

I had four weeks to think about this, before they came to interrogate me again. I existed in a state of nervous apprehension, feeling that they might come at any time. I hadn't thought I'd be left alone for so long. I was very careful about my appearance, afraid that, if they took me by surprise and found me looking untidy, it would hurt my vanity and my pride, and therefore put me at a disadvantage. I made up my face, went on dyeing my eyebrows and eyelashes every week, and wore the shabby trousers and sweater only at weekends, when I believed I was likely to be left in peace.

I didn't know about the Park Station bomb, nor that the police were fully occupied in investigating John Harris, who had placed it as a protest. It was a woefully misguided act, for passers-by had been killed and injured. Harris paid the harshest possible penalty, for the police broke his jaw when they beat him up during interrogation, and they finally sent him to the gallows.

I learned that I was at Gezina police station, on the outskirts of Pretoria. The cell was one of a row along the back of the station yard. Each of them, apart from the one that held me alone, held numbers of black prisoners, and each was behind its own small courtyard with high walls and locked door. Around the cell door, on the inside, was a large, box-shaped grille, like a cage, which the uniformed constables never unlocked except when they were accompanied by some senior officer, or by a woman. I suppose the barrier was intended as a protection for them, in case I attacked them, or accused them later of having tried to rape me.

The cell was large, bare and draughty; no problem with cross-ventilation there. There were plenty of windows, but they were all too high to look through, and there was no furniture to climb on. There was a bench bolted to a wall away from the windows. In the corner was a lavatory: the kind that is a hole in the floor, not the kind with a seat. On the concrete floor were four felt mats and some blankets. In this, I was privileged, since the black men who generally occupied those cells got only one mat and one blanket each. I was there because I opposed apartheid, but it still worked in my favour. In fact, the regulations prescribed bedsteads for white women, and the station commander told me I would have been given one, had there been any in the station at the time.

Walls and lavatory were filthy; the mats and blankets reeked of sweat. Each morning, when I got up, I saw my nightdress was grey with dirt. No doubt, I was grey with dirt too, but there was no mirror to show me. When I complained, I was told that there was no provision at the station for washing bedding or cleaning lavatories. This meant that short-term prisoner after short-term prisoner, year after year, used those blankets and lavatories, unwashed and unscrubbed. There was no tap in the cell either, and my water supply was held in several catering size instant coffee tins which, I suppose, came from the staff canteen, and which I filled, each exercise time, at a tap in the station yard.

A previous prisoner, who hadn't given his name, but who called himself an "ANC man", had kept his daily calendar on the wall behind the door, hidden when the door was open. He had recorded every day, from October 1963, over Christmas and the New Year, through the whole of the summer and the autumn, till June 1964. Solitary confinement was making me fanciful, and it seemed to me that his presence was there with me, in that cell, as an ally and a support.

There were compensations for the lack of physical comfort. I found the atmosphere of the police station less formal, more cheerful, than that of the gaol. As the only white woman in the place, I got special food, brought three times a day by a policeman's wife, and evidently from her own table: comforting mutton stews, with rice, potatoes, cabbage, pumpkin: Afrikaner home cooking, and infinitely better than prison food. The uniformed police were courteous, but here, again, I was privileged.

Once, during exercise time in the prison yard, I saw two or three white constables slapping a black youngster who couldn't have been much more than sixteen, and who was shaking all over with fear. "Waar's jou geld?" they were shouting, "Where's your money?" I'm sure he didn't have any money. Of course I knew that police habitually used a lot of physical violence against prisoners, but this display of brutality was in front of me, only two or three yards away, and I was deeply shocked.

I made a routine for myself. Breakfast came at eight, together with a zinc bucket of warm water. After I had eaten, I laid a folded blanket on the floor for my daily exercises and, when they were done, I washed in the bucket from head to foot. I then used the same water for washing my clothes, rinsing as best I could, over the lavatory, with what was left in the instant coffee tins. The next event was morning exercise time, half an hour in the sunshine in the station yard, under the eye of a policeman, who handed me my cigarettes and took them back when I returned to the cell. Then came the midday meal, followed, later, by another half-hour in the yard. By supper-time, as the winter evenings came down, I was once more in my dressing-gown. I used to sit on the edge of my bed, waiting for the policeman's wife to arrive with her dish of rich, homely soup, watching a patch of opalescent sky through the window, and reflecting, with some kind of satisfaction, that I had got through another day.

I asked for more buckets of hot water, and washed the walls of the cell, carefully leaving the ANC man's calendar intact. After many times of asking, I got a brush and disinfectant to clean the lavatory. Apartheid machinery ground on: a narrow, iron bed arrived, the mats were taken away, but the mattress was lumpy, less comfortable than the mats, and I still had the same blankets, with no sheets.

The only conversations I had during those four weeks were very brief. Constables unlocked the door now and again to find out if I was all right. The station commander came each morning to ask whether I had any complaints or requests. What a question! One morning, I replied, "Yes. I want to go home," and he smiled at my little joke.

Senior officers came from time to time to ask the same thing. Nobody ever knocked at the door before they opened it, but the noise of the keys being turned in the outer door of the small courtyard, and then again in the cell door, was ample warning.

I had a visit from a magistrate who came, according to the law, to inspect the conditions I was being held under. Everyone knew this was a useless exercise, for the magistrates reported to no outside authority, only to the Department of Justice which controlled the security police. This man spoke to me through the grille, while a constable stood by, holding the keys to the outer doors. He asked whether I had any complaints about my "treatment". I replied that I had been roughly manhandled at the time of my arrest, and that the police had refused to show identity cards or warrants. "I don't want to know about that," he said, "I'm asking about your treatment." "But that *is* my treatment," I replied indignantly. It may be that he was reluctant to convey to the security police my complaints about their misconduct. Perhaps such complaints were part of his daily routine, and he thought them not worth bothering about. Perhaps my manner alarmed him, for it may well be that I sounded shrill and looked wild-eyed. At all events, that was the end of the conversation. He turned away; the constable closed the door and locked it.

At weekends, my time in the courtyard was supervised by young policemen, sometimes by police cadets, who all kept their distance, and sometimes by the station commander himself. During the week, my guard was usually an elderly, uniformed sergeant, who was sorry for me. I don't think he'd have felt any sympathy if I'd been black, but I was a white woman, and sometimes he talked to me, in a fatherly way, when no one was watching. He meant well. Once, he said, "If I were you, I'd tell them what they want to know, and get out of there." He looked in through the open door of my cell which, from the bright light in which we were standing, seemed very dark and gloomy. "It's terrible in there," he said. I couldn't deny that, and so made no reply.

He still thought of Namibia as South West Africa, and referred to it in the way of his race and generation as "South West". He told me once about how he'd served there, in the days when the police there used camels more often than horses or motor vehicles. He described the methods they had used in dealing with cattle thieves who refused to tell them where the stolen cattle were. The rustlers were San people, whom he called Bushmen. The police would feed the suspects biltong, dried meat, very thirst-inducing, then tether them by the neck to a camel and ride the camel across the veld until the prisoner, dehydrated and exhausted, would gasp out the information they wanted. I was deeply shocked again, for this was an aspect of racial oppression and the torture of prisoners, that I'd never dreamed of.

It was a pleasure and a relief to talk to anyone, but my conversations with the sergeant were little consolation. I had nothing at all to read, for police stations don't have stocks of Bibles, and my ballpoint refill was of no use to me, for I had no paper. It seems incredible now, but I read the leaflet in the Tampax packet over and over again, for want of anything else. On most days, I rationed my games of patience to the time after supper, since I didn't want that joy to pall with too much use. I had been given the choice, and nine o'clock was the time I had chosen for the light to be put out. There seemed to be no reason for keeping it on.

Solitary confinement drives everyone slightly crazy. It induces loss of concentration, loss of memory; strange fancies and terrors; an intense fear of others, or else an intense desire to communicate with them. The desire to communicate can focus on the police, when there is no one else to talk to, and some people feel an urge to boast about their exploits to the police, when they have no one else to boast to. There is also an unfocused stare, which the prisoner isn't aware of, but which is visible to others.

I couldn't see myself staring, but I know I began to feel other effects within a few days. During the long spells when I wasn't otherwise occupied, I talked to myself nearly all the time, often very emotionally, putting into words everything that was happening to me, everything I was doing and thinking. I often found myself laughing one moment, and crying the next. All this time, I walked in circles round and round the cell. I didn't allow myself to sit or lie down during the day, except at meals or, paradoxically, during exercise time in the courtyard, where I would perch on an old wooden bicycle stand in the sun, and smoke. I wanted to tire myself out so that I'd sleep at night. I slept well, from soon after the light went out till just before breakfast, probably because of a combination of day-long walking and sheer boredom.

Before I was arrested, I'd thought I'd be able to keep my mind occupied in solitary by reciting poetry to myself, and by singing songs. I know a good deal of poetry by heart, and quite a few songs but, in that cell, I found the poetry had all gone, and so had the songs. When, after I had been there a month, a senior police officer lent me a Bible of his own, I found my concentration much diminished. I was quite unequal to the Book of Kings, and I read unmethodically, whatever seemed least demanding: the Book of Ruth, the Acts of the Apostles.

I had plenty of time to think about why I was there. In fact, I had begun my self-searching on that first afternoon of terror and anxiety. I had asked myself whether I'd made a mistake; whether I regretted any of my political affiliations and political activity. I thought it all through carefully, step by step, and found nothing to regret. There was no point in my life at which I could have changed my mind and stepped aside from the path that had led me to that cell. It was very simple: I couldn't accept the system of oppression in South Africa. Prison cells can't change opinions.

Later, in the United Kingdom, addressing groups on behalf of the Anti-Apartheid Movement or the ANC, I was often asked what had made me, and whites like me, break with our backgrounds in the way we had. I found the question impossible to answer. I had certainly broken with my background: a conventional white home, a school for white middle-class girls, where I had been bored and unhappy.

In fact, my sympathy with Communism had first shown itself at that snobbish, dreary and unstimulating school. I had read no Communist literature, and had never knowingly met a Communist, but I had read some of Dickens' novels, where the gap between wealth and poverty was most painfully described. I had also read Hewlett Johnson's *Socialist Sixth of the World*, and it seemed to me then that Communism had something positive to offer society. In my last year, when the topic for the English essay prize was announced as: "The Novel of the Nine-teenth and Twentieth Centuries as a Document of Social History", I wrote my essay with special reference to the Industrial Revolution, and the rise of socialist thought; and its climax was the Russian October Revolution of 1917.

I had not yet learned to relate any of these ideas to the situation round me, in South Africa; I saw them as European. In fact, I was as crassly naive and ignorant as any seventeen-year-old girl can possibly be, and it was a severe reflection on the quality of the other essays when I was awarded the prize by Geoffey Durrant, then professor of English at Natal University, to whom the essays had gone for adjudication. I was too naive then to understand why the award seemed so unpopular within the school, nor why the teachers received the news with stony faces and half-hearted congratulations.

Later, I'd been very happy at university, but it was a white university, and had turned out many white racists, and many who were racist but pretended not to be. People often react against their backgrounds, but I don't know why I chose radical politics. Why, for example, didn't I become a gangster? That, too, would have been a revolt.

The answer must have been partly, at least, to do with morality. The system in South Africa was wrong, profoundly immoral, and there was no denying it. Never was it easier to identify right and wrong, than it was in that situation. Those who struggled to change that system were right, and those who supported it were wrong. We were right to promote the cause of justice against injustice. I cannot account for the fact that so few whites saw that moral necessity.

Many years later, I was to read what Chris Hani had said about how he had become involved in politics. He was a brilliant and widely loved leader of the ANC and of MK, and had risen to become General Secretary of the Communist Party when he was murdered in 1993. He said he'd been influenced by the literature he'd studied at university, which had denounced tyranny, and put forward principles of equality, of respect for human beings. It's true that value systems in the greatest literature are based on these principles, and what I read certainly had an effect on me. I cannot explain why it didn't have the same effect on everyone who studied it.

In the course of this self-examination, I thought a lot about physical torture, and about how I might react to it. The possibility terrified me. I remembered reading about a political prisoner in some other country, who had been tortured and who had resolved each morning, "I won't talk today. I may talk tomorrow, but I won't talk today", and who, in this way, succeeded in getting through without talking at all. That seemed a good idea, and it was reassuring to have some sort of plan.

There, in isolation, I didn't know that the police had added another method of interrogation to beatings-up and electric shocks, until then their commonly used methods. They had begun to use sleep deprivation too, and were working in shifts, day and night, shouting questions and threatening, keeping the prisoners awake, and often keeping them standing for days on end. Inevitably, prisoners lost this battle.

Piet Beyleveld had advised us not to tell lies, but simply not to speak at all: "Don't try to be too clever. You don't know what other people have told them." It remained the best advice, though prisoners deprived of sleep, and exhausted by standing upright, always broke down eventually, and talked. Some deliberately made statements while they felt they were still clear-headed enough to keep those statements to a minimum. Sometimes they succeeded in keeping information back, and sometimes they didn't, because the police understood what they were doing, and demanded more detail and more truth.

CHAPTER 5

Interrogations and statements

Interrogations started again for me just before nine one morning in the middle of August. I had had my breakfast, done my exercises, had washed, and had begun to get dressed, when I heard my courtyard door being unlocked. I had time to get into my dressing gown, and the young constable who had been sent to fetch me was caught between his embarrassment at finding me dressed like that, and his fear of the security police detectives who had ordered me to be brought out.

The detectives were enraged at being kept waiting. Their display of temper was quite uncontrolled, and I could hear them yelling in the station yard. Their anger was directed against me, against the young constable and, it seemed, against the whole station staff, including the station commander, though, as a warrant officer, he held the same rank as the senior special branch man and outranked the others. When I finally came out into the yard, dressed, I saw that all uniformed men there, from junior constables upwards, were looking very strained. They were being treated with great rudeness, and were being accused of dereliction of duty in failing to produce me at once. The security police could get away with all kinds of threatening and intimidating behaviour.

I was taken away. No one told me where I was going, nor how long I'd be away but, as my bag and nearly all my possessions were left in the cell, I assumed I'd be brought back again.

This happened for three days running. Each morning, they arrived before I was dressed. Each morning, the shrieking and bullying was repeated because they never told me they were coming, and I don't think they could have told the station commander either, because, if they had, he would surely have tried to avoid the unpleasantness by seeing that I was ready on time.

They took me each morning to Compol Buildings, Pretoria police headquarters and, in a small, dusty back room, with a blind pulled down over its window, a number of men questioned me all day. Kurt Danziger's work had forewarned me about many of their methods.

Of the detectives I saw, there were three who seemed to have been assigned to me. I'd seen them before, during my previous, brief interrogations, and when I'd been moved. I spent most of the time at Compol Buildings with two of them. Those two took up the roles of the nice guy and the nasty guy: I'd heard about this ploy, and it is well attested to in literature as being a method used in interrogation by police all over the world.

The nice guy said he was Warrant Officer van Rensburg. I was pretty sure I recognised him as the man who had followed Ann and me that night on the bus. He was friendly, polite, gentle; complimented me on my appearance, urged me to make a statement and get myself out of the difficult situation I was in. The suggestion that a statement would get me my freedom was, of course, a lie: plenty of people who'd made statements had afterwards been charged and sentenced, and indemnity could be got only by giving evidence in court. Big-built, fresh-faced, with a certain charm, Van Rensburg reminded me a little of a man I'd once been in love with, but the resemblance wasn't strong enough to make me want to confide in him.

The nasty guy said he was called Geyser, and I think he was a sergeant. One of his tasks seemed to be to dispense unpleasant surprises, and he gave out scraps of information from time to time, to show me how much they knew. He also shouted, hectored, threatened, made insulting remarks: "Jy's vuil," he kept shouting at me at one point, "You're dirty." I think this was meant to demoralise me. He made racist remarks and anti-semitic remarks, too: one such was, "Tell me, Jean, what are you doing in a movement where they're all Jews, except the fools?" I suppose this was calculated to provoke me into some ill-considered reply. I remained silent, and detested the very sound of his voice.

The third man, small, skinny and sharp-witted, was the clever guy. His name was Grobler. I never learned his rank, but he seemed to be in charge of the other two, and in charge of other teams as well, and he didn't sit in on all my interrogations. I think they were all surprised when I showed a preference for talking to him. He was by far the most interesting to talk to, and, after weeks in solitary, I had an irresistible need for conversation, even for a battle of wits. I had to be careful though, for the situation was dangerous; prisoners have been trapped into saying more than they intended, by precisely this need to lock minds with another human being.

When they called me Kenna, I knew that Ludi was no longer their only source of information. It became clear that they now knew much more than Ludi had known, and more than I knew. It was clear that people had been giving information, and that Piet Beyleveld was one of them. He knew more than any of the rest of us. I have a feeling that he was in the building, finishing off his statement, while I was there, because Grobler kept coming into the room with more snippets of information to try out on me.

In the same way as I had tried to pretend not to be trembling when they arrested me, I then tried not to show my shock and dismay. It would have been a sign of weakness that they would have taken advantage of at once. I tried to sit quite still, and keep my expression as blank as before. I told them I'd discuss anything with them except political matters. I said I'd been reading the Bible, and was prepared to discuss it. Geyser, in a rare flash of wit, said, if that was the case, he'd be prepared to discuss Revelations.

They showed me Beyleveld's statement, a very thick document, but I put it aside, without glancing at it. We knew that the police sometimes faked statements to get information from other prisoners, and even if it were genuine, I needed to go on taking refuge in impassive behaviour.

They then showed me a handwritten diagram that removed all doubts from my mind. It took only a second or two to grasp what it was. It showed a segment of the Communist Party, from our units through the Johannesburg area and district committees, right up to the Central Committee. It looked something like a family tree: lines connected the groups, each group was represented by a box, and there were names written in each box. The handwriting looked like Beyleveld's. He had given away a whole segment of the organisation: everything he knew about the Party, and its membership. I put aside this piece of paper too, trying to seem unaffected by the sight of it.

I suppose they were trying to break me down when they showed me these things, though they must have known by then that they could get nothing new from me, except for a few details, and perhaps a promise that I would give evidence for the state. It wasn't too difficult to remain silent.

After I arrived back at the police station on the first evening, I overheard one young constable say to another, "Did you see her when she came back? Her face was grey. Grey!" Those day-long interrogations were an ordeal, but I was getting gentle treatment, compared with what some other prisoners were being subjected to. I slept in my cell each night, and they didn't use physical torture. I didn't stop being afraid they would though. One of the reasons I preferred being questioned by the clever guy was that his speciality was clearly not torture, but questioning. Of course I knew that, as soon as he thought it necessary, he would give the order for one or both of the others to torture me but, when I was actually in his presence, I felt safe for the moment.

On the third morning, when I felt I could no longer endure the crude Geyser, I said impatiently, "I can't stand any more of this. I want to speak to your superior officer."

They responded far more quickly than I'd expected. One of them left the room at once, and came back, and then they escorted me to another office. It was Grobler's. I realised they'd misunderstood what I'd said, and thought I was going to make a statement. However, the chair was comfortable, Grobler was offering me tea and cigarettes, and I took advantage of this for a while. He put a photograph of Lewis Baker in front of me. Again, I tried to pretend not to be interested, but it was another shock, and I was sorry too, for I'd hoped Lewis had somehow slipped through the net.

For a while, Grobler was friendly and chatty and, thanks to the preparation I'd had, I perceived landmines in his chat, and was able to avoid them. Then, he described various judges' rulings in some detail, and assured me that any statement I made could not be used as evidence in a court of law. At last, he politely asked me if I was ready to start making my statement. I answered, "Of course not. I never said I was going to make one."

He made his last threat. "I'm sending you back," he said. "You can sit fretting in your cell, and I can get on with my work." Fretting in my cell. That was a pretty good description of what I'd been doing.

They took me back to Gezina, and locked me in. All afternoon, and long after the light went out, I thought about what had happened, and its implications for the organisation and for myself. What we had built so carefully was smashed, and others would have to build again. Perhaps we weren't very important, but any damage to the underground meant some delay in the coming of democracy in South Africa. I ate steadily through the biscuits and sweets I had with me in the cell, and heard a distant clock strike ten, eleven and twelve, before I fell asleep.

I was moved the next day. Within ten minutes of being called, I was once more in the back of a Beetle, with the bag that held my clothes and cosmetics. There were no biscuits or sweets left. I also had a huge packet of detergent I used for washing my clothes, and which I carefully held upright as we swung round corners. The station commander had sent a constable out to do this shopping for me, using my money, and the constable had come back with the biggest packet I'd ever seen. He must have thought I was going to be in a long time.

When my police escort booked me into the little prison in Boksburg, I knew where I was, because the name was over the door. I thought at the time that the place must date back to the Transvaal Republic. Years later, in 1994, I read in the press that the old Boksburg Female Prison was no longer in use, but was being preserved as an historic building, like the Fort in Johannesburg. There was talk of turning it into a museum, even a restaurant, with coloured lights and "overnight accommodation". Perhaps it's possible that, under different circumstances, with a few coats of paint, with colour and comfortable furniture, the little room I occupied, with its tiny, sunny, whitewashed courtyard, shower and lavatory, might be a pleasant place to stay overnight, as a joke, if one wasn't locked in.

That room was a cell, then, and it was daunting. The walls were grey. The window looked on the courtyard, but was set so low that it let in very little light. There was the usual iron bedstead and flock mattress, grey blankets, and (because this was a prison, not a police station) sheets; there was a battered prison-issue wooden stool, a rusty sanitary bucket. The cell door was unlocked each morning, for me to spend the regulation hour out in the courtyard, with the courtyard door still locked, but most of that time was spent in showering and washing my clothes, and it seemed to me that, as soon as I'd settled down in the sun for a smoke, the wardress came to usher me into the cell again, and lock the door.

I was suffering a reaction from the days of interrogation, found the place oppressive, and was often in tears, when I was alone. Once, I tried to repair my morale by singing the Red Flag to myself, but stopped before I came to the end, because the part about dungeons dark and gallows grim made me feel worse. One day, I screamed hysterically at the doctor, for no better reason than that I thought he had given me the wrong indigestion mixture, and the matron of the prison advised me good-naturedly: "Don't fight with the devil in hell." Sitting on my stool at the window, with a mirror I'd been allowed to have, I discovered my first grey hairs.

The best thing about that time was an illustrated Bible, sent in by Ilse Fischer, daughter of Bram and Molly. I loved the pictures. One picture, that I looked at over and over again, showed Jesus at the moment of being arrested by a stern-looking Roman soldier, while Judas skulked nearby. It spoke to me of my own recent experiences, especially the grave and threatening look on the soldier's face. I found the concentration to read a little more of the Acts of the Apostles, and was thrilled by the story of the angel who rescued Peter from his prison cell.

One afternoon, when I'd been there less than a week, a wardress came to take me to the matron's office. There were two security branch men there, who told me to get my things together, as they were taking me to be charged. I said, "Good", because we had always asserted emphatically that prisoners should be either charged or released, and not detained without trial. They drove me to Marshall Square police station, which was police headquarters in Johannesburg before John Vorster Square was built. We drove there from Boksburg, so I never did travel back along that road from Pretoria.

At Marshall Square, I was brought together with others: Esther and Hymie, Flo, Ann, Sylvia, Pixie, Norman, Costa and Paul. We all felt tremendously elated and excited at being with people again. Esther and Hymie greeted each other rapturously, after their separation, but it was clear from Hymie's appearance that he'd had a bad time.

Sheila and Beverley weren't there. They'd been released, for the police had nothing substantial on them. Beyleveld wasn't there either. I said to Esther, "You know, I think they've got Lewis", and told her about the photograph. I said it very quietly, because the others weren't supposed to know that Lewis was involved with us. In fact, the police hadn't picked Lewis up yet. He was arrested coming out of court a few days later, and put in detention.

They took our prints: full prints, including the palm. They told us triumphantly that copies would go to Interpol; perhaps they thought we'd be frightened by the news. It was a long job, and while it was being done we were able to compare notes. I learned for the first time about sleep deprivation and the standing torture. It had happened to the men in our group, but not to the women. We were the last to be spared in this way; and I believe that, from that time on, the security branch did not discriminate in their treatment of prisoners under interrogation.

People made telephone calls to their families, and the news spread fast that we were being charged, and were therefore no longer detainees, but prisoners awaiting trial. Families and friends came that evening, with comforts that our new status entitled us to: books, magazines, newspapers. These served as messages of support, since the police station wasn't organising visits that night. Philippa sent in a book for me, which I tried to read, but I couldn't concentrate on it, couldn't make sense of the words.

We were locked up, men in one large cell, women in another. After weeks of having no one to talk to, Esther, Flo, Ann, Sylvia, Pixie and I exchanged experiences.

Flo had been in Pretoria all the time, in the same tiny, dark cell. I was full of admiration when I heard she'd defied the matron, and had stayed in bed all day, except for exercise times, since there was no point in getting dressed and making the bed just to spend the day sitting on a hard, wooden stool in the cold, and staring at the wall. She said she'd won the battle when, one day, during exercise, the matron screamed at her, and she'd screamed back. "It was her or me," she said. A wardress told her afterwards that she'd been at the tennis courts, and had heard the screaming from there.

Esther had been in Boksburg while I was in the Gezina cell and, when they had finished interrogating me and were ready to start on her, the police had swopped us over. They must have taken care to ensure we didn't see each other, for that might have given us courage.

Ann Nicholson had been in Marshall Square, and Pixie Benjamin in the Fort, all the time, except for a couple of nights – separately – in Newlands police station in Johannesburg. Each had found the cell at Newlands a frightening place, with black walls and, in the windows, broken glass covered with torn paper, which flapped all night, in the wind. They could hear the cries of a mental patient, who was being held in the cell next door, presumably for want of more suitable accommodation.

Both agreed the police had most likely hoped it would break their spirit. Ann had even refrained from complaining about it, since she feared this would act as an incentive to the special branch to leave her there. Smiling radiantly, she had told a visiting magistrate, "It's fabulous here! – and the food's wonderful." She thought she must have reasoned correctly, because she'd been moved the next day, back to Marshall Square. However, the astonished magistrate disapproved of a young woman with such low tastes, and said, "*My* daughter wouldn't like it here."

Sylvia had been in a police station, where she had been able to make contact with Ivan Shermbrucker, a detainee in a neighbouring cell. She said they had talked every night, and these conversations had seemed like a lifeline to her. Apart from telling us this, she was as unforthcoming about the details of her experience as she had been after her first detention, and gave no details about how she and Ivan had managed to talk to each other. She probably thought that if the police overheard what she said, and learned the method they had used to communicate, it might spoil the chances of prisoners yet to come.

We were continually aware – even in that cell at Marshall Square – that we might be in the presence of hidden microphones, yet if it occurred to any of us that the police might have deliberately allowed those conversations between Sylvia and Ivan, and had listened to them, we didn't discuss it, even when we were out of the cell. I think we may all have been too confused at the time to reason it out. That evening, we heard that, for a few days, Pixie had had another detainee as a companion in her cell at the Fort: Norma Kitson, wife of David Kitson of the "D" group, who was himself in detention then, and who, a few months later, was sentenced to twenty years. Cell-mates were unheard of in ninety-day detention, for solitary confinement was the basis of the system, yet the security branch, who placed their prisoners so carefully, had countenanced this. Pixie was enthusiastic about how much she had enjoyed Norma's lively wit. The police must have hoped that one or both of them would say too much, in their joy at having someone to talk to.

A few months later, it became public knowledge that the police were recording conversations in cells, when tape recordings were brought as evidence against a common-law prisoner who had spoken too frankly to his cell-mate. However, we heard nothing more about what Sylvia and Ivan, Pixie and Norma had said to each other, so it can be assumed that they had all been discreet in matters where discretion was necessary, and that if the police had, indeed, been trawling, they had trawled in vain.

I don't know what we felt most strongly when we saw Pixie: admiration or shock. She was dark, with strong features; vivacious, strong-willed, often bossy. She was always thin, but, by that time, she was emaciated, very pale, physically terribly weak, and still refusing to give up the hunger strike we had begun in Pretoria Central. Sheila had fasted for twenty-one days and Esther for thirty-five. Pixie, had continued for forty-nine days, and still wasn't eating, insisting that she wouldn't touch food till she was charged or released. That evening, she got undressed, very slowly because she was so weak. She looked like a skeleton. We stood round her, awed. "You look terrible," we said. We meant this as praise of her courage, and that was how she took it.

The rest of us had felt that food would keep up our strength, but Pixie's source of strength had been the stand she was taking. "Don't sabotage me," she said sharply to someone who suggested she eat something to keep her going through our appearance in court. She refused supper that night and breakfast in the morning, and took her first mouthful only after we had been formally charged.

We had been in detention fifty-three days. It had seemed a long time, but it wasn't long compared with the terms some others had been through. Quite a few, like the ANC man in the Gezina cell, had gone into their third term of ninety days, and Alfred Nzo had gone into his fourth. Probably, it was Pixie who had saved us further time in solitary. It later became clear that we had been charged prematurely, before the police had got all their evidence together, and it was generally believed they had acted hastily, to prevent her death. That would have been an embarrassment to them.

The next morning, we were taken to court, and charged with membership of a banned organisation. Joel Joffe, the attorney, had come to represent us. He looked pale and anxious, and at once secured a consultation with us in an airless little lock-up beneath the court.

He had only one question to ask us, at that stage: whether we knew someone called Ed Round. He didn't speak the name aloud, but wrote it down on a piece of paper, which he showed to us. None of us had heard the name before; we all looked blank, and Joel looked relieved. We later learned from the newspapers that Ed Round was a provocateur who had trapped Marius Schoon and Raymond Thoms, both former members of the COD. He had asked them to join him in placing a bomb at the Hospital Hill police station, as a protest something like John Harris's, only directed specifically against guardians of apartheid, in the shape of the police force. When Marius and Raymond arrived at Hospital Hill, carrying their components of the bomb, Ed Round wasn't there. Instead, there was a contingent of police waiting for them, led by Colonel Fred van Niekerk.

There were ten of us: Esther and Hymie Barsel, Pixie Benjamin, Florence Duncan, Constantinos Gazides, Norman Levy, Sylvia Neame, Ann Nicholson, Paul Trewhela and myself. We weren't asked to plead, and most of us made no bail application. Pixie was the exception; she applied on the grounds of ill-health after the hunger strike. She wore a warm purple jersey someone had sent in to her, because she thought the corpse-like appearance the colour gave her might help her case. It didn't help, and her application failed, because the prison doctor was brought to testify that the cell we were to occupy was a "hospital cell", and she'd be taken care of. We were all remanded in custody, and taken to the Fort, which was then the Johannesburg prison.

One good thing happened to me that afternoon: an indirect message from a valued friend. Someone sent us in a copy of the Johannesburg *Star*, and I glanced through it while we were waiting for the prison van to arrive. I wasn't able to read much, but my eye was caught by a photograph on the letters page. It was of Geoffrey Durrant, who had awarded me the school essay prize, and who had subsequently taught me for five years at the University of Natal. I managed to concentrate on his letter. He had written from Saskatchewan, to protest against the arrests and detentions in South Africa. He said that he knew some of the young people who had been detained, and they were both intellectually and morally superior to their captors. So slow was my reasoning that day, that it took me some time to grasp that he was writing about me, among others, but, when I did, I felt a glow of gratification.

CHAPTER 6

Awaiting trial

We spent our first night at the Fort in a row of six single cells. They were very tiny, but not too oppressive, for each had a sash window, barred but large, that let in a lot of light. When we were locked in, we found the beds made up, by other prisoners, with clean sheets, and clean prison nightdresses folded under the pillows. The nightdresses were warm and comfortable, and not unsightly, being made of blue and white-striped winceyette, and cut like long-sleeved, knee-length shirts. I climbed into my nightdress, then into my bed, and was soon asleep, exhausted.

The next morning, we were flung from solitary into overcrowding. There were two large cells in the white women's section, and we were all moved into one of them. Each had a little lawn with a flower bed, and there was a wall between. They were arranged one on either side of an administrative room known as the "surgery", probably because one of its functions was to provide consultation space for the doctor, when he came.

Perhaps its proximity to the "surgery" was the doctor's justification for having stated under oath that our cell was a "hospital cell". Nothing else about it suggested a hospital. It was about as big as a middle-sized living-room. It was the cell that, a short while before, had held Pixie on her own and, for a few days, Norma Kitson as well. Now, it held six women, their beds, their small bedside cupboards, a small table, and a wardrobe. There was a washbasin and a lavatory in the corner. When we were locked in, we sat or lay on our beds, for there wasn't enough space for us all to move about at the same time, and certainly no space for chairs. We were to spend eight months there.

Our trial was only one of many that arose from the mass arrests of July 1964 and, during the second half of the year, the police were kept busy bringing cases to court. We didn't come up till November. Except for one or two brief court appearances for remand, and one or two visits to the dentist under security branch escort, we spent the time from late August till mid-November in the Fort, day after day. Spring arrived, the mornings came earlier, we heard the dawn chorus of the birds (wherever it was they sang, in that place), but we were in a cell in the Fort. For the first few weeks, we couldn't even begin preparing our defence as the police hadn't produced an indictment.

Mollie Anderson was still free when we were charged. She and her husband were staying in the Benjamins' house, helping John look after the children, and Pixie had had a letter from her, giving her news of her family. Then she too was arrested, and brought to join us at once, without a period in detention. This brought up to seven the number of women, beds and cupboards in the cell. Mollie's arrest was a particular wrench for her, as she'd been married only a few months, but she refrained from complaining much about this misfortune, and she was like a fresh breeze blowing from outside, with news and gossip. She had even done a mailing she told us secretly, on the grass outside the cell. She'd posted off leaflets single-handed, using addressed envelopes and stamps, all hidden away just before we were arrested.

Because of the six months she and Pixie had served the year before, for slogan-painting, they were more experienced in the ways of prison than the rest of us. They were both remarkably strong and cheerful, considering they were facing their second sentence in two years, together with suspended sentences from the slogan-painting charge.

Within a few weeks, there had been more arrests, besides Mollie's, and more names added to the list of accused. After waiting outside his house for days, as a visible presence, the police finally arrested Bram Fischer. They also arrested Ivan Schermbrucker and Eli Weinberg, neither of whom had been in any of the area groups.

Ivan had been involved in politics since his days in the army in World War Two, and had worked for the succession of left-wing papers, beginning with the Communist Party *Guardian*, which had continued under different names, through repeated bannings, till 1961. I had come to know him slightly when I had worked in Durban for *New Age*, one of this series. I had met him in underground work once in Johannesburg when, introduced by Esther, he had passed a large package of leaflets to me before a distribution. In one way or another, we all knew Eli, both as an activist and as a person, but I don't think any of us knew Ivan very well, if at all. I don't think Sylvia had known him before they became acquainted in detention.

Lewis Baker was brought out of detention and put in the Fort with the other men. He was a gentle person, and loved his family. When I saw him in court, he told me he'd suffered hallucinations in solitary confinement, had been convinced he'd heard his wife, Villa, sobbing in a nearby cell, and had frantically and repeatedly called to the warders to give her attention.

Those of us who had been in detention took time to get over its effects. Pixie had to make a physical, as well as a psychological, recovery, so she took a bed next to a window, between the bars of which, every four hours, wardresses handed her a nourishing drink prescribed by the doctor. She soon went on to solid food, and began to put on weight. We all talked compulsively, incessantly exchanging accounts of what had happened to us, what we had done, the policemen who had interrogated us, what they had asked, and what they had said. I looked at pictures and cartoons, and it was weeks before I could read. My state of mental disorganisation got badly in the way when I tried to write letters, for my handwriting, never good, was almost illegible and, worse, I found it difficult to articulate a train of thought. I was embarrassed by the letter I wrote to Geoffrey Durrant, but it was the best I could do at the time, and so I sent it.

The number of letters allowed for prisoners awaiting trial was unlimited, but they had to get past the prison censor. A friend living in the United Kingdom wrote to me: "Describe what it's like there. What are your cells like? What are your beds like? What about your cell-mates?" I had to reply that the descriptions she wanted were just what I couldn't give, because we weren't permitted to write about prison conditions, or other prisoners. If this rule was broken, sections of the letter would be blacked out, or the letter would simply never be sent.

We had a letter from Hilda Bernstein, who was by that time in London, with her husband, thankful that they were together again. Before he had left the court, after his acquittal in the Rivonia trial, he had been rearrested, on charges similar to ours. Out on bail he had decided that his nerve was going, he couldn't stand any more, and wanted to leave the country: a wise decision, since I dare say he still knew a lot about what was left of the underground organisations. We were surprised we didn't hear from any of the other Communist Party leaders in exile. We learned afterwards that they'd been afraid they might incriminate us.

We began to get letters from strangers overseas, people who'd responded to an appeal from the Anti-Apartheid Movement, to write to political prisoners in South Africa. These letters gave us great encouragement, and discussing and writing replies that were acceptable to the prison censors, helped to keep us occupied.

Visits took place on Tuesdays and Thursdays, in a room divided by two wire-netting screens, with a space of three or four feet in between. Visitors went in from the entrance hall, and prisoners from a courtyard. A wardress stood behind the prisoners, and another behind the visitors. Four or five prisoners at a time stood in a row to take their visits, and everyone shouted, in an effort to be heard above the din. Lucy, Elena and Wolfie came to see me when the schools were closed, and brought me things I needed. Philippa used to come, and, on one occasion, brought with her a sympathetic teacher from the private college, a visit they combined with one to Norman, on the men's side.

Helen Joseph came to see me once. I understand she had refused more than one invitation to join the Communist Party, and I heard she'd been very angry when every member of the national executive of the COD, except herself, had been, in one way or another, revealed as a Party member; "I was the fall guy," she was reported to have said. We'd never thought of her as a fall guy, only as an asset to our executive committee, and I was very pleased that she'd recovered from her anger enough to visit me.

Pixie and Mollie said the gaols in Nylstroom and Pietersburg were far more comfortable than the Fort, and that Kroonstad was known to be the most comfortable gaol of all. We hadn't shared their experiences, and preferred the Fort to Pretoria and Boksburg, the only other gaols we knew, as distinct from police stations. The white section was old and slightly ramshackle, which gave it a relaxed air. The commanding officer of the women's prison was loud and autocratic, but had some sense of fairness, and was more sophisticated than the "matrons" we'd known earlier. With the rank of lieutenant, she was the only woman commissioned officer any of us ever encountered in the prison service.

Her elder sister, a former nurse, was the wardress in charge of our section. Reasonable, fair, unshockable, with a sense of humour and a sense of when to turn a blind eye, she was quite unlike any of the other wardresses we ever met, before or after. Once, after some cigarettes had been found illegally concealed in our cell, we overheard her say, without rancour, "Prisoners can always hide things from us. They've got nothing else to think about all day." Our quarters were cramped and it was a tedious time but, thanks to her, the atmosphere in that section was not unpleasant.

We had to observe the formalities of prison, like standing to attention to be counted, when our cell door was locked and unlocked. There was a rule forbidding smoking in the cell, since the place was rightly regarded as a fire hazard, but all prisoners broke that one, whenever they had the chance. We had to hand our cigarettes to the wardress before we were locked up, but by that time we always had a cache or two hidden away, to see us through the evening. One of the best places was under the leaves of a potted plant just outside one of the windows, for it was easy to stretch an arm between the bars, and retrieve the little package, after the wardresses had gone off duty. Another place was on the flat, horizontal surfaces of the highest transverse bars of the tall sash windows. Mollie was very imaginative in thinking of hiding-places, while I was the only one tall enough to carry out her ideas, so, when they discovered our caches, the wardresses used to think the ideas were mine. "That Middleton's clever," one was overheard to say, as she carried some confiscated cigarettes away with her. Matches were more difficult to get hold of, for the wardresses would often give us a light but keep the box. Some evenings, we had to keep the light going by lighting from each other, and smoking in turn.

We had to keep our cell clean, which meant crawling on our hands and knees under and between the beds, to sweep up the dust from a roughly-finished floor with a broom head that had no broomstick (a complete broom might have served as a dangerous weapon), and washing the windows with wet newspaper, polishing them up with dry newspaper. These duties done, we spent most of the day outside our cell, on the grass or walking up and down a little path. We were locked in at five, and then we would eat, read, play chess or Scrabble, and smoke. We did all this on our beds, for it was impossible to use the table, which already held our plates, mugs, cutlery, and the food lavishly provided by our families and friends. After the lights went off at eight, we lay on our beds in the dark, telling each other the stories of our lives.

We were all middle-class white women but otherwise, I suppose, we were a mixed bunch: a commercial traveller, a radiographer, a teacher, two students, a sales assistant, a housewife. We were aged between twenty-four and thirty-nine. Common values, common interests and, later, common experiences, bound us together. To this day, those of us who remain – Pixie died of cancer – are still in touch with each other, and our relationship now is probably best described as being something like that between sisters, compounded of loyalty, affection, exasperation, and deep familiarity.

The experiences I shall describe from here on are those of this group of women. This is simply the reflection of those experiences, of what our lives were like. Throughout our time in gaol, we were kept apart from other prisoners. Black and white women were held in different sections of the prison, and governed by different regulations: black prisoners got no bread, for example, only samp and mealie meal porridge, and didn't get meat every day. We used to smuggle our uneaten rations of bread through dark, barred windows to black women in the big main building, but never saw them, except when they were brought through to do some menial work in the yard on the white side.

The authorities tried to keep us apart from common-law white women prisoners too; not, I think, to protect us from their influence, but to protect them from ours. Despite the wall, it was difficult to separate us though, in that small white section, so we often got to speak to them. They perceived us as "educated", like the women in for fraud, who were at the top of the social order in prison, but I'm glad to say they told us that, unlike the fraud prisoners, we didn't "put on airs".

Above all, women prisoners were kept apart from men. After the trial began, we sat in the dock with men, and shared the trial with them, as we had shared the political work we were being tried for, but so strictly are men and women segregated in gaol, that we shared no other experiences. We were held in the "female section" of the Fort, while they were in the "male" prison next door. We had senior and junior counsel to defend us, but no joint consultations – counsel visited first one section of the gaol, then the other. We were taken to court in separate vans or separate sections of the same van, and kept in separate cells below the court, when we weren't in the courtroom.

Throughout this time, Esther and Hymie were obliged to discuss their children, their house, and their money problems, in letters. On the days when we went to court, they weren't able even to eat their sandwiches together, and, in the prison, the wall between male and female sections divided them as effectively as if they had been hundreds of miles apart. They applied to visit each other, but this was refused, on the grounds that, as there was no communicating door between the sections, one of them would have to be conducted along the pavement in Kotze Street, and back again. The prison authorities claimed to be short-staffed, and therefore unable to provide the necessary escort.

The divide was deep, but sometimes the men, apart from Hymie, wrote to us across it, as their women comrades. Eli wrote, giving us the words of some stirring trade union songs. There was a lively letter from Costa. It seemed he had a very low professional opinion of the district surgeon who acted as prison doctor; justifiably low, we knew, for the doctor didn't seem to take much interest in his patients. Costa used quotation marks to get his opinion past the prison censor, who missed their significance: "I have seen the 'doctor'," he wrote. I wrote to Norman, teasing him about the fact that, though we were almost exactly the same age, the newspapers had him down as ten years younger.

The monotony of those days was broken by two attempts at escape. One was by Sylvia. Delicately-boned, fair-skinned, pretty, with a mass of curly blonde hair, she looked the picture of fragile femininity, but she could be as stubborn as Pixie, and even more single-minded. When the security branch put her in the back of a four-door car, to take her to the dentist, she opened the door at a traffic light in Hillbrow, and ran. She had purposely worn flat, rubber-soled shoes, in case the chance should come up. She was athletic and could run fast, but one of the policemen could run faster. He sprinted after her and brought her down with a rugby tackle. She was taken back to the prison, put into one of the small solitary cells for a few weeks – the usual punishment – and then brought back to join the rest of us. She took it all quite stoically.

The other escape was a more professional job, conceived and executed by a gangster named Gertie: young, bright, attractive, with a long criminal record and a history of escapes. My giant box of detergent had a part in the incident. It stood on our lavatory cistern, next to the washbasin, and could be seen from the door and windows. We later learned that the sight of it had given Gertie inspiration, for she had persuaded one of the prisoners awaiting trial to get a friend to send in a similar box, with hacksaw blades buried in the washing powder. She was being held in the other large cell and, on the night of her escape, the other prisoners remained behind, having less to gain by the risk. After she had gone, they shouted the alarm, as they were obliged to do, if they weren't to be accused of aiding and abetting her. We heard the shouting, and we heard the prison siren go off. Next morning, a senior wardress questioned us about a skipping rope Ann and Flo had been using to keep fit, for it seemed Gertie had used it to help her over the wall.

She was recaptured later, by which time she had got pregnant, and couldn't run so fast. She then underwent severe punishment for months, in solitary, in one of the tiny cells, with only a mattress, blankets, and a prison nightdress. After the lights went out, we used to make up parcels of sandwiches, sweets and biscuits, and persuade a friendly young wardress on the night round to deliver them to her, between the bars of her window. She was still in the Fort when we left and we heard no further news of her or her baby.

There were two other common-law prisoners we had some contact with, because they were trusties, prisoners who had special privileges, and what passes for responsible jobs in gaol. One was called Tessa, and, while we were there, she went to court after a ten-month period awaiting trial, and was sentenced to a year. She helped the wardress in charge to dispense medicines, rations of our own cigarettes, and other controlled goods, from a locked cupboard in the "surgery". It seemed she spent so much time in the Fort that she knew this job well, and was re-assigned to it whenever she arrived back in, even while she was still awaiting trial. She didn't seem to be able to run her life outside very well, being continually charged with petty offences like burglary, theft, soliciting; but, inside, she was efficient, responsible: a trusty.

She enjoyed the books we lent her, but thought us very simple-minded. Once, she heard me say crossly, "*Why* can't I have my eyebrow tweezers with me in the cell?" After a slight pause, during which she decided I was quite serious, she replied, in a patronising voice, "You can pick locks with them, dear." I hadn't known that, so she was right in thinking me naive. We enjoyed her dry sense of humour. One morning, I complained to her, "It's raining again," and she replied, "It can rain all year, if it likes. I'm not going anywhere."

The other trusty, a very different kind of person, was Laura. Laura had everything – a good job as a bookkeeper, children, and a husband who visited her regularly. She was good-looking too; the only woman I ever saw who looked really good in the unbecoming prison uniform of the time, without make-up, her uncut hair in a French pleat at the back. Her work outside was her undoing, for she couldn't resist lifting the money she handled, and she was doing a five-to-eight-year sentence, which meant a third offence. She had paid a lot of money for the "outside" clothes she had with her, and which we saw her wearing when, later, she was moved to the gaol in Kroonstad. Her work as a trusty inside gaol brought no temptations, and was easy: it was looking after the "front", that is, dusting the furniture in the hallway and in the Lieutenant's office, and arranging vases of flowers on the Lieutenant's desk.

The "front" was the scene of a scam carried on by a very young prisoner, who was awaiting trial towards the end of our stay. It seemed she always had a supply of cannabis, to help her space out during the long, boring evenings in her single cell. Through the grapevine, we heard how she got it. In the hallway, opposite the Lieutenant's office and next to the visitors' entrance to the visiting room, was a small, polished cabinet, under which her visitors would drop a small parcel, as they filed into the visiting room. Later, as she waited to see the Lieutenant on some pretext, standing to attention, hands behind her back, according to the rules, she would surreptitiously stoop and pick it up.

We weren't all Lauras. Clothes, and grooming in general, became a problem. Our hair and nails were becoming unmanageable. After an urgent request to the Lieutenant, we were allowed to use nail files and nail scissors, but only under the eye of a wardress, who had to take time out to give us these things, watch us as we used them, and then lock them up again, in the "surgery" cupboard. Tessa wasn't trusted with this job. Ann trimmed our hair, as best she could, with a pair of scissors, also from that cupboard.

As spring came and the weather turned warm, we sent our jeans and sweaters out of the prison; friends and families sent in what was left of the previous summer's cotton dresses. There was no need for new ones, for we were sure it would be a long time before we were out again. Flo sent out for the overalls she had worn to work as a radiographer, and shared them with those of us who were the right size. I remember the pink one I appropriated.

We began planning what to wear to court. The Communist Party had been banned for nearly fifteen years, and we felt that, in the media and in popular mythology, communists figured as maladjusted, unreasonable and dangerous, different from ordinary, decent people. Looking presentable in public was a matter of pride. We were going to wear high-heeled shoes, sheer stockings, our most elegant dresses and appropriate jewellery. By then, it was far too warm for the grey flannel dress I had had with me in detention, and for the coat and skirt I had asked Lucy and Elena to send in for me to wear at the second remand, but I had two summer dresses I decided were good enough, and someone outside – I never knew who – supplemented these with the gift of a third.

The indictment, when it was eventually published, was dispiriting, because it had material facts right, about meetings and underground structures. I lost the position of accused number one, a status symbol I was happy to do without. Bram was named as the first accused, Ivan as number two, and Eli as number three, and they were named as members of the Central Committee of the Communist Party. Norman, because he had done some service on the district committee, was number four. The rest of the area committee followed: Esther, Lewis and I. After that, came the group members. The trial became known as the trial of Bram Fischer and fourteen others.

Not unexpectedly, this period of strain and apprehension was a time when some of us did our own thinking about whether we were on the right course. Most of us were exploring ideas that should have been familiar to us, but weren't, because, in underground conditions, we had had little opportunity to study and discuss political principles. An ideological disagreement arose over the usefulness of the Communist Party. Some argued that, if it hadn't existed, we wouldn't be in gaol, but would still be politically active. We could be communists, they argued, without the Party, and they thought we should smuggle out a report recommending its dissolution. The opposing argument was that we had more power if we were united in collective action, that the Party was a place that enabled us to discuss just what it meant to be a communist, and what policies we should adopt. The argument finally died down and, if the minority recommendation for dissolution was ever sent, I didn't know about it.

We heard that Piet Beyleveld was to give evidence for the state. This was terrible news, that shocked and disturbed us very deeply. Becoming a state witness was regarded as the most reprehensible, the most treacherous, thing a comrade in the underground could do. It was destructive to the underground organisations. It also meant that someone was getting indemnity by putting comrades away in gaol, perhaps for many years. We had learned to accept the reality of statements made under duress in detention, but in open court there was no duress, no torture, and to give state evidence was thought of as unforgivable.

Beyleveld would get his indemnity and his release only after he had given evidence, and if the court regarded his evidence as satisfactory. We heard he was in Gezina police station. It was likely he was being held in the same cell that had held first me and then Esther. I reflected angrily on how I'd unwittingly cleaned up that cell for him, by washing the walls and disinfecting the lavatory. I wondered how he felt at the sight of the ANC man's calendar.

We bore up, in spite of these blows, because life became more purposeful. We had begun to see where we stood, and where things were going. It had become clear that Ludi, too, was to be an important witness, for the indictment was confined to a period of about a year, beginning when he was recruited and ending not long before our arrest. Although we hadn't yet heard the evidence, it was possible to begin planning a defence.

Defence was difficult. Bram had no hope, for he had both witnesses against him: Beyleveld from the Central Committee, and Ludi from the unit. I was in the same position, because I had worked with both at some time during the period of the indictment, and this went for most of the unit members, though, in the case of some of them, the period had been very short; only a few weeks, before Beyleveld was moved, after the Rivonia arrests.

Ludi had never known Eli, Ivan, Esther, Norman, Lewis, Hymie, nor Pixie, as members of the Communist Party. There was only Beyleveld's word against theirs.

All the accused agreed that anyone who had a chance of getting off was fully justified in lying, doing whatever they could, taking whatever chance they had. We were conscious of the moral implications of this. We believed that the racist regime was immoral, and that it had no legitimacy, because it was undemocratic; elected by a minority; was kept in place by force and violence, and not by consent. It followed that we didn't believe its courts had any legitimacy either; no right, moral or otherwise, to try people and sentence them, especially political opponents. Therefore, as the police and the courts sought to put good people in gaol, we believed in putting in their way all the obstacles we could.

Plans began to develop: those with a chance should go into the witness box in their own defence, deny membership, and suggest that Beyleveld was manufacturing evidence in order to gain indemnity. Counsel began to coach them.

Pixie never had to go into the witness box. On the first day of the hearing, charges were dropped against her, and the fifteen accused became fourteen. This was because of a technicality, for, though she had worked with Beyleveld in the Communist Party, it had been before the period of the indictment began. She went home and, a few weeks later, looking plump and beautiful, came to visit Flo during an adjournment. Also on that first day, Hymie was granted bail, a sign that the state expected an acquittal. He could go home, bring the three girls home, and was able to visit Esther from then on. He and Pixie and their families had all undergone unnecessary suffering, because of the intransigence of the prosecution.

Bram got bail. The state could hardly avoid granting it to him, for he had to go before the Privy Council in London, to plead a case in which he had been involved for some time. He didn't seek political asylum in Britain, as he might have done. He returned to South Africa after the case in London was over, and in time for the beginning of our trial, which he attended for a few weeks, until soon after the Christmas adjournment.

I think it was at this time, during an adjournment, that he paid us a lawyer's visit in the women's section of the Fort: an excuse for a chat. He looked sad and serious, and somewhat untidy. His grey hair needed cutting, and his clothes didn't fit him well. When he stepped through the doorway, and was outlined against the light, I saw for the first time how much weight he had lost. The thought crossed my mind that he might be planning to go into hiding, and this might be part of a disguise he was preparing for himself. At the time, I didn't express the thought to anyone. We were well trained in keeping our mouths shut.

I suppose he meant that visit as a leave-taking, for, one morning early in January, he didn't turn up in court. Counsel announced that he had disappeared during the night. He had left a cheque for the bail money, and a letter, in which he explained that he intended to remain in the country, and go underground to work in the struggle for freedom.

More than thirty years later, in 1996, I met Maggie and John Bizzell, who were part of the team that arranged the disappearance. They told me the loss of weight had been planned and supervised, so my guess had been right. Bram was to become slim and dapper, with dark hair. A Danish comrade, Raymond Schoop, and his wife, Diane, had been in the team. Raymond had learned much from his partisan family as a youngster in the days of the Nazi occupation, and had worked on Bram's appearance, with new false teeth to change the shape of his cheeks, and strategically placed lifts inside his shoes, to change his walk. Someone in the team took a house in the name of Mr Black, the name Bram was going to adopt. Mr Black was a photographer. He was also a widower and, as part of his legend, they supplied him with pictures of fictitious children, from whom he was supposed to be estranged, a school background, and a war record.

On the morning Bram disappeared, John Bizzell drove him into the Magaliesberg mountains, not far from Johannesburg, and left him there, in the house of an old friend. He hid there for a while, and then, having changed his appearance, returned to Johannesburg, to occupy his new house and his new identity.

I think he'd been afraid that the rest of us, denied bail and held in prison, might feel he'd had an advantage over us, and resent it. The reality was quite the opposite. We were delighted at what we saw as his victory, and we felt we shared in it. Margaret Smith, the journalist, reported in the Johannesburg *Sunday Times* the following weekend that the accused in the dock had been "jubilant" at hearing that Bram had got away. What she said was true. We heard afterwards that she'd made a point of saying it because she knew that, somewhere, on that Sunday morning, Bram would be reading the *Sunday Times*.

CHAPTER 7

Trial

Ours was the longest trial that had ever been heard in the Johannesburg Regional Court, and it was a busy and exhausting time for us, in spite of our somewhat passive role. We were up before seven, having breakfast, having thermoses filled in the "surgery", making sandwiches, and getting dressed. Soon after seven, we were escorted to the Lieutenant's office, where we stood in line, waiting to have our thumbprints taken and to sign for our watches and money, and such jewellery as we had with us. This was according to the rules. The thumbprints were for identification, in case of attempts to substitute other people in our place. Our money, watches and jewellery were issued to us in case we were released during the day, though Pixie was the only one of us who'd had the slightest chance, and we knew well there would be no more releases after hers.

When the van arrived to fetch us, we were handed over into the custody of uniformed policemen, and a police "matron", who stayed with us throughout the day. The accused in political trials never travelled with other prisoners. The journey to court was sometimes terrifying. Presumably, the police feared attempts to rescue us. We could see enough through the barred windows to know that they were driving us at breakneck speed, and with little respect for stop streets. There was one driver whom we called the "kamikaze"; we joked about his being a fascist so dedicated that, in destroying us, he was prepared to immolate himself.

Jean Middleton in London, London, 1971. (Photo: Ann Nicholson)

Lewis Baker, c. 1963. (Photographer unknown)

Sheila Weinberg (wearing a hat) gives the Congress salute of that time, a clenched fist with a raised thumb. On her left is Barbara Harmel, daughter of Rae and Michael Harmel, both well-known communists and activists in the Congress movement. Violet Weinberg, deep in conversation, is third from the left. Early 1950s.
(Photo: Eli Weinberg)

Esther and Hymie Barsel in their garden, mid-1970s.

Violet Weinberg with her daughter, Sheila and son, Mark. Mark used his father's timing device to take this family picture for Eli in prison.

Eli Weinberg: a self-portrait taken after his release.

Sylvia Neame and Jean Middleton, Berlin, 1982 (Photo: Gerhard Jahn)

Mollie Anderson and her brother, Ewald, 1964 (Photo: Eli Weinberg)

"Communists," say 5 Fischer trial accused

FIVE OF THE 14 ACCUSED in the Fischer trial today made statements from the dock admitting that they were Communists.

The trial is now in its 49th day in the Johannesburg Regional Court.

The main figure in the trial, Abram Fischer, is still missing after jumping bail of R10,000.

Soon after the proceedings began this morning, 2,000,000 words were recorded—a record for the lower courts in South Africa.

The five who made statements from the dock were Jean Middleton, Ann Nicholson, Constantinos Gazides, Paul Trewhela and Florence Duncan.

Middleton said:
"I admit that I was a member of the Communist Party and on an area committee. After the verdict has been given I will tell the court why I became a Communist."

She would not go into the witness-box as she would be required to answer questions under cross-examination which might reveal the identity of people she was associated with.

"I am not prepared to do this."

Ann Nicholson told the court: "I do not deny that I was a member of the Communist Party. After I have been convicted I will tell the court why I adopted these views."

Constantinos Gazides said: "I also do not deny that I am a Communist. I attended two Communist Party cell meetings. I attended one a month before my arrest."

Paul Trewhela said "I am a Communist and member of a cell. Most of the evidence against me is factually true but the inferences are wrong. I expect to be convicted."

Florence Duncan also admitted that she was a group member of the Communist Party.

DOYLE'S DENIAL

Doyle told the court that she was most certainly not a Communist. She was a member of the Congress of Democrats.

She said she agreed to a suggestion by Middleton to address envelopes for leaflets. In carrying out this task she was very cautious as she had served six months in prison in 1963 for putting up posters for the A.N.C. (a banned organization).

"I used gloves as my fingerprints were known to the police, and I disguised my handwriting."

(Proceeding)

POLICE TELL OF MORNING RAID ON GIRL'S FLAT

COURT REPORTER

AN early-morning raid on the flat of Jean Middleton, an alleged Communist, was described in the Johannesburg Regional Court yesterday by one of the men who took part in the raid.

Lieutenant Gert Janse van Rensburg was giving evidence on the twelfth day of the trial of Abram Fischer, Q.C., and 13 others all of whom have pleaded not guilty to charges under the Suppression of Communism Act.

Lieutenant Van Rensburg said that at 6.30 a.m. on July 3, this year, he went to Middleton's flat in Santa Barbara, Ockerse Street, Hillbrow, with Lieutenant-Colonel Van Niekerk and another officer. He said they knocked on the door and told Middleton, who inquired through a window who they were, that they wanted to see her.

GOT KEY

After a "long" interval during which he heard the toilet flush twice, he got a key from the supervisor and opened the door. Middleton tried to stop him at the bathroom door, but he went through to the toilet because he suspected that she was trying to get rid of certain documents. He found nothing there.

Lieutenant Van Niekerk said that he and his colleagues then searched the flat and took possession of certain articles.

At this stage of his evidence, the hearing was adjourned to Monday.

Earlier, Sergeant Christian Petrus Kleingeld, of the Security Branch, Pretoria, the man who was in constant contact with secret agent Gerard Ludi, described watching certain slogans being painted. He said he had received information from Ludi and other sources that the slogans were going to be painted.

SLOGAN

Questioned by Mr. I. Mohamed, for some of the accused, Sergeant Kleingeld said that "Free A.N.C." — a slogan that was painted on a wall of The Fort — was an appeal to lift the ban on the African National Congress. Sergeant Kleingeld said he knew that people had agitated on these lines but said he did not know if there was still agitation.

Mr. J. H. Liebenberg, of the Deputy Attorney-General's Office, with him Mr. A. O. S. Maree and Mr. W. P. Theron is appearing for the State.

Mr. H. Hanson, Q.C., with him Mr. C. Plewman, instructed by Bell, Dewar and Hall, is appearing for Fischer.

Mr. V. C. Berrange with Mr. I. Mohamed and Mr. D. Kuny, is appearing for Schermbrucker, Weinberg, Esther Barsel, Baker, Middleton, Doyle and Hymie Barsel.

Mr. Kuny is appearing for Nicholson, Gazides and Duncan and Mr. Mohamed for Trewhela and Neame.

All are instructed by Hayman and Aronsohn.

WHAT THE CASE IS ABOUT

THE CASE INVOLVES 14 PEOPLE CHARGED UNDER THE SUPPRESSION OF COMMUNISM ACT WITH BEING MEMBERS OF THE COMMUNIST PARTY, TAKING PART IN THE ACTIVITIES OF THE PARTY, AND FURTHERING THE AIMS OF COMMUNISM.

THEY ARE ABRAM FISCHER (56), IVAN FREDERICK SCHERMBRUCKER (43), ELI WEINBERG (56), ESTHER BARSEL (40), NORMAN LEVY (35), LEWIS BAKER (54), JEAN MIDDLETON (26), ANNE NICHOLSON (24), CONSTANTINOS GAZIDES (28), PAUL HENRY TREWHELA (23), SYLVIA BRERETON NEAME (76), FLORENCE DUNCAN (31), MOLLY IRENE DOYLE (29), AND HYMIE BARSEL (44).

Newspaper reports of Jean Middleton's arrest and trial.

Molly Fischer, 1964.
(Photo: Eli Weinberg)

Bram Fischer, 1964.
(Photo: Eli Weinberg)

REPUBLIEK VAN SUID-AFRIKA   REPUBLIC OF SOUTH AFRICA

Verw. Nr./Ref. No.:   C 26(11)

KANTOOR VAN DIE—OFFICE OF THE

NAVRAE/ENQUIRIES:

Tel. No.:

Magistrate,
GERMISTON.
4th September, 1968.

Miss. Jean Middleton,
19 Shelley Avenue,
Senderwood,
JOHANNESBURG.

Madam,

With further reference to your letter of the
14th August, 1968, you are hereby granted permission
to leave the Magisterial district of Germiston on
the 12th September, 1968 to travel to Durban, subject
to the following conditions:-

(a) that you are in possession of the necessary
departure documents;

(b) that you report you departure from Germiston
at the Bedfordview Police Station and your
arrival in Durban at the Berea Police Station;

(c) that you travel directly from Germiston to your
mother's residence in Durban and that you remain
at this address until your departure from the
Republic on the 18th September, 1968;

(d) that on the 18th September, 1968, you report your
departure at the Berea Police Station and travel
directly from your mother's residence to the Durban
harbour to depart from the Republic; and

(e) that you adhere to your restriction notices in
all other respects.

Yours faithfully,

CHIEF MAGISTRATE/GERMISTON.

*Letter from Germiston
magistrate's office to Jean
Middleton, stating the
conditions of her trip to
Durban from where she
left for England on
18 September 1968.*

REPUBLIC OF SOUTH AFRICA.

OFFICE VAN DIE—OFFICE OF THE
MAGISTRATE,
PRIVATE BAG 4308,
DURBAN.
September, 1968.

Dear Madam,

With reference to your letter of 11th
September, 1968, and subsequent telephone calls,
I have to advise you that you are hereby permitted
to visit a hairdresser and a commercial bank, subject
to the following conditions:-

(a) that the hairdresser is situated
in African Life Arcade , West Street;

(b) that your appointment is made
during normal business hours;

(c) that your financial business be
undertaken at a commercial bank
in West Street opposite African
Life Arcade;

(d) that you have only one appointment
with the hairdresser;

(e) that if it is necessary to make more
than one visit to the bank this office
is advised prior to the time of
leaving;

(f) that you enter town by the normal bus
route and proceed direct to your
destination; and

(g) that you do not contact any banned or
restricted persons.

Yours faithfully,

JM

Acting MAGISTRATE : DURBAN

*The letter from the
Durban magistrate's office,
16 September 1968,
granting Jean Middleton
permission to go to a
hairdresser and a bank*

One morning, we on the women's side felt we'd had enough, and, when called to the transport, sat on our beds and refused to move. Within a few minutes, a group of uniformed policemen appeared round the corner, picking their way across the grass and round the flower bed, towards our cell. They were our escort, and had come to take us to the van by force. We made what we hoped was a dignified retreat from our position, by demanding from the senior officer an undertaking that we'd be driven safely. He gave it. I think there was relief on both sides that the matter had been peacefully resolved. Throughout all this, the "matron" remained carefully neutral. She was part of the police team, and so owed it her loyalty, but she, too, had found the journeys unnerving and, on one or two occasions, had even screamed with fright.

From the van, and still heavily guarded, we used to enter the vast, gloomy basement beneath the court building, and were locked up behind bars till the time approached for the day's hearing to begin. Then we were taken to the cell below the courtroom where our hearing took place, and the men were brought from their cell to join us. The door was locked and guarded. Just before ten o'clock, we were called to file up the stairs that led straight into the dock. We spent the midday adjournment in the first cell, and the procedure was repeated in the afternoon.

Back in the prison, we had to stand in line again, to have our thumbprints matched up with those of the morning, and to hand in our money and jewellery. Outside our cell, on the verandah by the garden, we had to strip to our underclothes, while our handbags and every garment were searched. Wardresses sometimes searched the cell while we were at court, and then bedclothes, nightdresses, little possessions from bedside cupboards, were strewn everywhere. So cramped were we for space, that we had to take it in turns to make our beds and put things away.

The weather was hot. Food sent in by friends, working in turns, would be waiting for us. Once in the cell, we longed only to collapse on our beds with our plates of dinner, but the short time left before lock-up was the only time when we could have a bath. We were spared having to wash and iron our clothes, for we didn't have access to sinks or ironing boards. Washing and ironing was done by sentenced prisoners, during the day, as part of their work.

The most exhausting part of the day was, of course, listening to the evidence.

We were charged with having been members of the Communist Party, and having furthered its aims and objects, during the period specified in the indictment. It was a complex task for defence counsel, as the case against each individual had to be considered separately, and the needs and interests of one group had to be balanced against those of another. The veteran Vernon Berrange was head of the defence team at the beginning of the trial, and Bram was represented by Harold Hansen, but Berrange withdrew from the case after a few weeks, and Hansen withdrew when Bram estreated bail. This left the exacting job to Ismail Mahomed and Denis Kuny.

It was a small group of advocates who handled the defence in all political cases in Johannesburg during those troubled and fearful days. George Bizos, Denis Kuny, Ismail Mohamed and David Soggott were the core. Joel Joffe and Ruth Heymann were the only attorneys. All carried an awesome load of work and responsibility, and much of the work usually done by the instructing attorney had to fall on the shoulders of defence counsel. Although he was formally our attorney, we saw Joel only once after our first appearance, for he was tremendously stretched, and what time he had for visiting prisoners was spent with those facing the possibility of life sentences or the death penalty, or those already sentenced to death.

These lawyers were paid by the Defence and Aid Fund in London, but no money could have fairly compensated them for the seriousness and sincerity they brought to the job, the friendship and sympathy they gave to those they were defending, or the sacrifice they made of their time and their other work.

When we were first asked to plead, we all pleaded not guilty, though we were all, in fact, members of the Communist Party and had all furthered its aims and objects, and though most of us knew we would have to plead guilty in the end. We were acting in accordance with Vernon Berrange's advice, and in accordance with our decision about telling lies in court: as apartheid was morally wrong, so was the Suppression of Communism Act, and we weren't prepared to give the security police any help in putting us away. Writing about the trial now, I am obliged to use words like "guilt" and "innocence", but I dislike doing so, because of their moral connotations. There could be no moral guilt attached to membership of an organisation opposed to the brutal and exploitative system that prevailed in South Africa then.

The prosecutor opened his case with a speech about what cunning, dangerous people the accused were. He quoted as an example a copy of *Fundamentals of Marxism-Leninism*, which had been found inside a brown paper cover, labelled *Fundamentals of English Syntax*. With a shock, I realised he was talking about me. That book had been taken from my shelves. I was dangerous, it seemed. I was to be more and more surprised by the way the prosecution presented us, as the trial went on.

He then led the first witness, who was Piet Beyleveld. Beyleveld had an excellent memory, and of course he had an excellent understanding of the nature of the Communist Party, of its policies, and of the political issues involved. He testified that he had been a member of a unit, of area and district committees and, later, of a central committee that had been put together after the arrests at Rivonia had disabled the previous one. He described the personnel and the activities of all these structures. His evidence was detailed and consistent, and he was telling the truth. He was in the witness box for a day and a half.

The accused sat appalled at this betrayal by someone we had trusted. In the COD, on committees and in the unit, we had liked and respected him as chairperson. To some of us, he had been a friend. We looked straight into his face throughout that day and a half, trying to stare him down and shame him. He remained calm and firm-voiced, and didn't seem afraid of throwing an occasional glance in our direction. His eyes had the distant, unfocused stare of someone who has been in solitary, so he didn't meet our eyes directly, but he didn't avoid them either.

We were amazed beyond words when the prosecutor read aloud a passage from the Programme of the South African Communist Party, and asked him, "Did you believe this?" and he replied clearly, "Yes. I still do." Under cross-examination by Vernon Berrange, he said he'd been made to stand while being interrogated, but hadn't stood for long, because he'd decided to make a statement. At times, we couldn't understand what he thought he was doing there in the witness box, giving evidence, except it was clear that, at this rate, he was certainly going to get indemnity.

Later, through intermediaries, we heard something of what he had said for himself. He said the police had confronted him with the threat that, if he didn't give evidence, there was someone else who would. According to this account, the other person was Bartholomew Hlapane, who had already given evidence for the state in the Rivonia trial. I don't think Hlapane was able to give significant evidence in our trial, but he was probably able to incriminate Beyleveld; in one of the big MK trials coming up, in which people were facing sentences of twenty years and more. It was clearly in Beyleveld's interests to accept the offer the police made him, and join Hlapane in the witness box, so to speak, instead of remaining in the dock.

When Beyleveld and Hlapane gave evidence, there was one point on which they disagreed. Hlapane tested to a close identification between the Communist Party and MK. Beyleveld flatly denied it; it was the only occasion on which he bent the truth. Other courts chose to believe Hlapane; the magistrate hearing our case found Beyleveld a reliable witness, and believed him.

Evidence of a connection with MK would have put our trial into a completely different league, with possible sentences of ten years on each count. Two lists the police had taken from the "D" group safe house, could have proved dangerous for us. When they were handed in as evidence, I could see them clearly from my seat in the front of the dock, and I remembered them well. One was in my handwriting, the other came from my personal typewriter, and they were names and addresses for the mailing list, that I had collected from my units, copied out and passed on, according to our rules. When the safe house was raided and they were all arrested, the "D" group hadn't yet made their own copies.

Because the "D" group had worked for MK as well as for the Communist Party, those mailing lists showed a connection, but police and prosecution ignored it. From the beginning, they had treated our case as a lower-penalty case. They hadn't taken us to the Supreme Court, but to the Regional Court, where a maximum sentence on each count was laid down. Perhaps this was part of the deal with Beyleveld. It's unlikely we'll ever know for certain.

Beyleveld knew well what we all thought of people who turned state witness. Possibly the prospect of indemnity and freedom had helped him to convince himself he couldn't do further harm by helping the prosecution in our trial, and he might even be doing some good by getting lower sentences for some, or all, of the accused. In all events, neither he nor Hlapane were granted indemnity at once. They gave evidence in other trials – notably, Beyleveld testified in the trial of the "D" group – before they finally got their freedom. Indeed, Hlapane was still testifying in the mid-seventies, when he was killed. It was believed that an MK unit killed him.

Ludi came next, introduced to the court as a warrant officer in the security branch. It wasn't clear how long he had been a policeman. Possibly, he had been recruited before he began to draw close to the COD, possibly after that, when faced with charges on some minor political counts, possibly just before the trial began. Rumour had it that, some time before, he'd been having an affair with a girl who wasn't white, and some believed that the police had discovered it and made a deal with him then, for such liaisons were against the law. Cross-examining him, Vernon Berrange probed for this, because, if the defence could have shown that the police had put him under pressure, Ludi's credibility would have been in question. We never found out for certain.

Once, when Vernon Berrange taunted him by quoting an absurd passage from one of his love letters, Ludi hit back, and angrily told the court that, in the line of duty, he'd had to go to "naked orgies" attended by members of "the left movement". This made headlines in the Johannesburg *Sunday Times*, which failed to mention that, under further cross-examination, Ludi had admitted he'd never seen any of the accused at these orgies.

We were outraged. However, when Elena and Lucy came to see me during an adjournment soon after, they couldn't contain their amusement. They both had a robust sense of humour; our corner of the staff room had been a lively one. "We never thought we'd read about you in the papers as the Christine Keeler of Johannesburg," they said, laughing heartily. Christine Keeler was a British whore of the early sixties, who'd had a high-class clientele, and who had been at the centre of a much-publicised political scandal. I found it impossible to share their joke, and looked at them sourly. However, the picture Ludi had given was so unlike the reality of the busy, serious lives we remembered leading that, after a few days, the accused all began to see a comic side, and this gave rise to jokes, like: "Why didn't you invite me to any of your naked orgies?" and: "Did your orgies start after I went home?"

Ludi testified for three days: an account of a succession of over sixty small unit meetings. It was suffocatingly boring, and Ann and Costa, hidden in the back row behind us, spent the time playing chess with a small travelling chess set. Ludi said his account was based on his memory, assisted by the notes he had made after each meeting. He described one meeting just before Christmas 1963, where I clearly remembered he hadn't been present; I dare say it was difficult for him to admit to his superiors that he'd gone to some party instead of doing his job. It wasn't worth our while to contest his evidence, since it was substantially correct.

A third witness was a baby-faced, young security policeman named Klaus Schroeder, who had been planted in the flat next to mine about six months before we'd been arrested. He seemed to be an immigrant, since his accent was German, not South African, and I'd sometimes seen him wearing *lederhosen* in the lift or on the landing. He looked far too young to have been in the Nazi Party, but I'd been sure he had neo-Nazi sympathies, because I'd once heard him playing the Horst Wessel Song on his record player. South Africa at that time might well have seemed a friendly and comfortable place for neo-Nazis. I hadn't suspected he was a policeman.

He had put dark glass in the transom above his door, and it seemed that, for several months, he had regularly climbed a ladder to watch comings and goings, unseen. From time to time, while I was out, he had entered my flat to plant microphones; transcripts of his tapes, bound in large volumes, were handed in as evidence. The court set aside a day on which the accused, together with prosecution and defence counsel, were taken to another, larger, cell below the court to hear the tapes, in case we should want to contest them. We didn't contest them, because they were, in essence, correct, though there were a few ridiculous mistakes in the transcription.

Schroeder had done a lot of work, and looked very proud of it, but, boiled down, his evidence didn't amount to very much. He gave names of people whom he'd seen calling on me, and dates and times when they called, but it meant little, since the people concerned, people like Ann, Flo, Mollie, Paul, Sylvia, Piet, Philippa, Marius Schoon, visited me openly; there was no secret about it.

His transcripts didn't advance the case much either, for they yielded little or no information about the underground organisation of the Communist Party. This was because of the precautions we had taken. Mollie was the only one materially affected, for she was on record describing how she had experimented with disguise, and the court ruled that this was evidence of her membership. We had been recorded quoting aloud from a Party document about the use of disguise. We'd never said aloud that the document was from the Party, but Ludi testified it was, and the two pieces of evidence, taken together, pointed to Mollie's membership.

More often than not, these solemnly reproduced conversations were ridiculously trivial. Marius Schoon came to sell me an insurance policy. He was no longer teaching, and we joked about the stress of work when we had taught together, on the same staff, saying that, when the government changed, white supremacists should be sent for punishment to teach at that school. Philippa and I once reminisced about a time when I'd babysat for her, and the child had screamed all evening. At another time, Sylvia came in while I was playing my recorder; "What are you doing, Jean?" she asked, and I replied, "Practising my recorder. Listen, I'll play *Where'er You Walk*." I was even on tape as saying to Flo and Piet, one Sunday morning, "I'm boiling my kitchen cloths", and this wasn't a code of any kind; I *was* boiling my kitchen cloths.

Of course, there were some conversations we would have preferred had remained private. For example, someone was deeply embarrassed because she was on record as saying, when she came in, "Jesus Christ, Jean, I hope I'm not pregnant." For the most part, though, they were not germane to the case.

Great emphasis was given to the names of all people mentioned on the tapes, whoever they were, whatever their connection with us. During the course of all those conversations, most of them purely social, it was only natural that many names of friends and acquaintances should come up, and each time one did, it was printed in capitals in the transcript. This gave the effect of an extensive conspiracy, and gave the impression that any friends whose names we happened to mention were part of the conspiracy, though some weren't members of any political organisation at all.

Apart from the tape recording about Mollie and the Communist Party document, there was very little corroborative evidence against those who had a chance of getting off. A minor witness told the court that she had once lent her sitting-room to Esther, for a meeting. Another, brought straight from his solitary detention cell, said he knew Lewis Baker and had sometimes discussed politics with him. Pressed by the prosecution, he said that Lew was inclined towards left-wing, rather than right-wing, opinions. Lew was very pleased. I gathered, from what he muttered next to me in the dock, that this man was, indeed, a member of the Communist Party, one of Lew's contacts, and was showing loyalty and ingenuity in giving innocuous evidence.

I think the police were intent on showing off their skills, and the state intent on demonstrating what desperadoes communists were. Evidence for the prosecution took many weeks, yet the state could have achieved its purpose with only part of the evidence it presented. The small pieces of corroborative evidence I have described may or may not have been material to the case but, essentially, it was the evidence of Beyleveld and Ludi, who had known us as members of the Communist Party, that secured our convictions. Most of the rest – including most of Ludi's tedious recital, and Schroeder's tapes about kitchen cloths and insurance and pregnancy – was redundant, unnecessary, especially where it concerned those like myself, who had no hope of being acquitted, anyway.

One example of this overkill was when the state subpoenaed Michael Bell of Terry and the Boys. Most of the accused didn't know Terry and the Boys, but those of us who did were surprised to hear Mike's name called, because we knew he hadn't been in detention. When he was asked to take the oath, it was the prosecution that was surprised. He refused to testify. He gabbled his speech in a voice squeaky with stage fright, for he wasn't a practised orator, and was not yet twenty years old, but he nevertheless proclaimed with resolution that he was not prepared to give evidence against the accused, because he agreed with what they were doing. We looked at him from our seats, with admiration and pride.

The court adjourned briefly, and counsel consulted us over the parapet of the dock. We insisted Mike should be asked to testify. He'd made a fine gesture, and declared his political stand, but he couldn't add anything to the weight of evidence against us. Ann and I both knew that the evidence he was able to give was about slogan-painting, and the court had already heard about that. We didn't want him to spend a year in gaol, and that was the penalty for refusing to testify. Our message was taken to him, and he was persuaded, gave his evidence, was dismissed by the court, and withdrew.

I heard long afterwards that he had asked his brother Terry, who was then starting on his career as a journalist, to compose his speech for him. "I want to tell them to fuck off," he said, "but I want to say it lekker."

Although Schroeder's evidence wasn't very important, either politically or legally, it was horrifying to me, personally. Knowing that he had watched me through that window every time I went through my door, had entered my flat, placed microphones, listened to every word I said, except those that had been whispered in the bathroom (we had rightly assumed the bathroom was safe), was an emotional shock that haunted me for several years. When we listened to the tapes, I could hear that the microphone had been under the coffee table at one time, and under my writing table at another, and that meant he'd entered my flat more than once.

I was even filled with embarrassment and misery during the few minutes when accused, defence counsel and prosecuting counsel, all sat in silence listening to my recorded performance of *Where'er You Walk*, though there was nothing to be ashamed of in the performance, which was correctly played and properly phrased. I felt as if it would never come to an end. Denis Kuny, who played jazz piano in his spare time, leaned across to me while it was going on, and said comfortingly, "It's nice, Jean." This made me feel a little better, but it was hard to bear the revelation that Schroeder and, through him, the whole Security Branch, the teams of lawyers, the court itself, had invaded my personal life without my knowing,

Schroeder was in court every day, all smiles, proud of his achievement. He used to stand in front of me, smiling at me, waiting for me to greet him. I don't know what he expected me to say: "Hello, Klaus, congratulations", perhaps. Perhaps he wanted me to burst into tears. In fact, I ignored him throughout the trial; simply looked through him, and then away. It was Flo who spoke to him, towards the end. She wasn't pleased either, at having had her conversations recorded, transcribed and bound into books. "You!" she said to him angrily, as she walked past, "All you're good for is sitting up on a ladder, like a monkey on a stick, spying on people."

Christmas came and went, providing some kind of break. In 1996, I read in the press that the former South African army general, Magnus Malan, who was on trial for murder, but out on bail, was being flown home at the taxpayers' expense, to spend the Easter adjournment fly-fishing. I thought of the hot, crammed cell at the Fort, where six of us spent the Christmas adjournment of 1964.

Everyone knew our next few Christmases weren't going to be very enjoyable, and friends outside tried to cheer us as best they could. Mona Nicholson, Ann's mother, sent in delicious Scottish dishes, chosen by Ann from her mother's repertoire, and huge salads of mixed vegetables. Connie Anderson, Mollie's mother, sent in a home-cured ham from the farm, and fruit salads laced with alcohol. Once, she went too far, and the prison authorities sent the salad out again; the wardress who had inspected it said, "When I opened the dish, the smell hit me in the face." Lucy and Elena sent in meals; Hymie's mother, and others, sent in fruit, nuts, chocolates. With little to do but lie on our beds and eat, we all put on weight.

The court reconvened early in January 1965, and the trial continued its slow course. Towards the end of the case for the prosecution, Ann, Flo, Sylvia, Paul, Costa and I changed our plea to one of guilty. Bram would no doubt have had to do the same, but he had gone by then. Counsel told us to begin preparing for the plea in mitigation that would be put to the court before sentence was passed. Ivan, Eli, Norman, Lewis, Esther, Hymie and Mollie prepared to go into the witness box.

When the defence opened its case and began to call its witnesses, Ivan, as accused number two, went first. He said he'd never been a member of the legal Communist Party, nor of the illegal one either, and that, in fact, he wasn't a communist by conviction. Those of us who had pleaded guilty had no quarrel with this, as far as it went. We were surprised and perturbed though, when he began to sound as if he had some contempt for the Communist Party, whose self-confessed members were sitting in the dock with him. Perhaps he was intent on playing his part well, and having the court believe him, and so was carried away by his own performance. Perhaps Ismail Mohamed was carried away by the hope of securing at least one acquittal, for, when he led Ivan in evidence, he encouraged him, suggesting that he was too intelligent and substantial a person, too upright a citizen, to have joined such an organisation.

In mitigation, we planned to take the line that we were intelligent, humane, principled, substantial people who had joined the Communist

Party because it stood for justice and democracy. Both accused number two and his counsel seemed to be undermining our argument, not to mention the good name of the Communist Party. If we had been consulted beforehand, we would have suggested some modification to Ivan's line of defence. When we saw the way his evidence was going, we wrote him a letter, urging him to remember the dignity of the Party, but by then it was too late for him to change course, even if he'd been prepared to.

It's surprising we didn't have more rifts than we did, for there had been no opportunity for discussion between the men and women accused. At the beginning, while still in a state of confusion and shock, the women had accepted Vernon Berrange's suggestion that the line of defence in the trial should be decided by accused one, two and three. I presume that the rest of the men had agreed to this as well. Of course, it was a mistake; we should all have taken part in deciding on our own defence; but we had committed ourselves, and the line of defence was being decided at meetings in the men's gaol.

The men and women accused had never once been able to sit down together, with or without the defence team, to talk about how we perceived the trial, its political significance, what image of the Communist Party we wanted to promote through the full, though somewhat biased, coverage we were getting in the press, nor what degree of defiance we should show, and in what ways. Within both groups, a kind of consensus was achieved, a kind of agreement on different points, a synthesis of differing views; but, between the groups, any divergence that existed must have grown wider as time went on, without our being able to check it. At that time we were seeing little of the lawyers, who were spending every possible moment on the men's side of the gaol, coaching those there who were trying to get off.

Eli followed Ivan. His defence was that, though he had been a member of the legal Communist Party of South Africa, and though he had remained a convinced Communist since its banning, he had not joined the illegal South African Communist Party when it was formed, and was still not a member. When questioned about the theory of Communism, he expounded it at length, with such sincerity, such enthusiasm, such eloquence, that the trial began to feel like a political rally. Our spirits lifted, and we were very proud of him, but we were pretty sure that he'd talked his way straight into a prison sentence.

Esther, Norman, Lewis, Hymie and Mollie all defended themselves in turn, with varying degrees of spirit, conviction and plausibility. They questioned the value of Beyleveld's uncorroborated evidence. They all freely admitted that they were democrats, and, those who had been members of the old legal Party admitted that fact as well, but they all denied membership of any illegal organisation.

We used this part of the trial to test our suspicions that our cell was bugged. I announced clearly in the cell that I was going to go into the witness box. I didn't make this statement anywhere else. Esther used to provide me with opportunities for repeating it, always in the cell. From time to time, during the ensuing weeks, she'd ask, in a clear voice: "What are you doing now, Jean?" and, without looking up from the novel, or the newspaper, or whatever it was I was reading, I would reply just as clearly, "Preparing my evidence to go into the witness box." As a test, it worked. When the last defence witness stood down, and the defence told the court that it was calling no more witnesses, the prosecution table was clearly confounded. Counsel conferred in whispers, and then asked for an adjournment so they could prepare for the next stage of the case. Our suspicion was confirmed: they had expected me to go into the box. Those microphones may well have been in the cell since the time Pixie and Norma had occupied it together. We had always assumed they were there, and had had all our important conversations outside on the grass.

We – that is, the women – began to sing in the van going to and from court. Most of the time, we sang *Shosholoza*. We sang quite loudly and very badly indeed, but we sang for political reasons. We believed it should be known on the streets of Johannesburg that there were political prisoners, resisters to apartheid, being driven in those closed vans. This led to another rift with the men.

Perhaps they didn't understand our reasons for singing, and explaining was too difficult, when we had so little time to speak to them. They didn't object because the singing was unmusical, though Eli, at least, must have found it very painful to listen to, but because it was militant. Eli wrote to us, saying it was unwise, because it displeased the authorities, and would lead to reprisals against us all, once we were serving sentences. We were disappointed in them, and went on singing.

The magistrate gave his verdict early in April. Beyleveld had been a good witness, and the court believed him, except in the case of Hymie, who was the only one to be acquitted. His acquittal was a great relief to both him and Esther, and, indeed, to all of us, since it meant he would be able to keep their home going.

Argument in mitigation came after the verdict and before sentence was passed. We had been preparing our statements for months. For those of us who hadn't gone into the witness box, this was to be our only opportunity of speaking our minds in open court, the only chance we were going to get, of putting our point of view. We wanted the statements to be as strong and as impressive as we could make them.

We wrote by hand, as the use of typewriters wasn't permitted in the prison, and we had to write while lying on our beds. We thought deeply, wrote and re-wrote, and handed the finished manuscripts over to counsel for the defence, to be typed. The typescripts came back to us, and we changed, corrected and improved them, re-writing some passages over and over again.

Political prisoners customarily used argument in mitigation to make political statements, not to get lower sentences. We knew that what we were going to say was unlikely to win the sympathy of the court, but that wasn't what we were trying to do.

Once, during a consultation, I told Ismail Mohamed that the statement I was writing might well get me a longer sentence than I'd have got otherwise. He smiled, and told me a story about how he'd once defended Nana Sita, the brave and highly respected Indian Congress passive resister. He had persistently defied the Group Areas Act, by refusing to leave his home in an area that had been designated white, and had been gaoled over and over again. On this occasion, Nana Sita had demanded counsel to defend him, and insisted on being heard in mitigation. Ismail Mohamed had argued hard to get the magistrate to agree, and then, after all this fuss, Nana Sita had asked for the maximum sentence. In his statement in mitigation, he had told the court: "Only the maximum sentence could be a measure of my contempt for the Group Areas Act."

Our statements were highly individual, but they all told the stories of our lives, and of how and why we had moved close to the Communist Party and then joined it. They were furious condemnations of the unjust and racist structure of South African society. They were defiant. They expressed no regrets. On the contrary, our arguments were, in general, that we had been more than justified in joining the Communist Party, since it sought to remove apartheid; that our opinions were unchanged and were unlikely to change; that we believed the laws of the country were wrong.

There was a week's adjournment before sentence was passed, so we had time to sort out our affairs. I had given up my flat. Elena and Lucy had given notice some months before on my behalf, paid the rent, packed up the contents, and arranged for them to be stored. In the Fort, we had to pack and send out all the things we wouldn't be permitted to have as sentenced prisoners – books, writing materials, tins of sweets and biscuits, all but the most basic cosmetics, clothes.

We were allowed to keep two good outfits, summer and winter, in case we were taken out of the prison for any reason. Convicted prisoners wear prison uniform, and their own clothes aren't left in their possession, because they would come in useful in case of an escape. They are given their own clothes to wear while they are being moved from one prison to another, which is how we came to see Laura's elegant and expensive outfit the day she was moved to Kroonstad. There is always the possibility of further charges too, and prisoners are handed their own clothes if they are taken to court again. I know of this last rule being broken only once, when Nelson Mandela, while serving his first sentence, was brought from prison in his prison clothes, to be joined with the other accused in the Rivonia trial.

We were taken to court to be sentenced on the afternoon of Monday, April 12th. We were sentenced on more than one count, but parts of the sentences were to run concurrently, and the effective sentences ranged from one to five years. Ivan and Eli got five years, Norman, Esther, Lewis and I got three, Ann, Mollie, Sylvia and Paul got two. Costa, who had attended only one unit meeting, got one year. These were the usual sentences being given at that time in cases like ours. We had learned from the newspapers that West German courts were handing out similar sentences to former guards in Nazi extermination camps, and we weren't certain which country this fact reflected on more unfavourably: South Africa or the German Federal Republic.

The magistrate left the court, we raised our fists in the air, and Eli led us in a defiant freedom song. The police, doing their best to put an end to this demonstration, began to hustle us out of the dock and down the stairs. I was gripping the dock rail with my left hand, found Schroeder next to me, trying to prise my fingers up, and, in the heat of the moment, freed myself with a karate chop to his wrist. Another policeman pushed me out of the dock, backwards, so hard that I would have fallen backwards down those concrete stairs from top to bottom, had I not succeeded in grabbing the stair rail, with an awkward hand, just in time. We were hurried to the van at once.

It was over. The men were taken directly to Pretoria, where quite a large group of white men political prisoners was being assembled. We were taken back to the Fort, strip-searched, and locked in the same cell we'd left at midday. Everything we were wearing, everything we had with us – clothes, shoes, handbags, jewellery, make-up, cigarettes – was packed in plastic bags and taken away to be locked in some cupboard.

The cell looked very different, for it had been cleared by a work party of other prisoners, while we were away at court. I hope they managed to secrete some of the food for a feast after lock-up. Our bedside cupboards were empty of all but soap, towels and toothbrushes; there was nothing on the table but six plates of prison supper. On subsequent nights, the wardrobe would hold six very ugly prison dresses, khaki with green collars and cuffs, but, on this first night, it was still empty.

Our status had changed again. We were sentenced prisoners now, subject to all the pettiest regulations. While addressing, or being addressed by, any member of the prison staff, we had to stand up, with our hands behind our backs. There were no newspapers, no books, no Scrabble, no chess, no cigarettes, and, for the time being, no more visits and no more letters.

As if to emphasise the bleakness, the weather had broken, and it was rainy and cold. We lay in bed, that first evening, in our striped prison nightdresses, and gazed at each other. I remember the black shadows under people's eyes. We had long ago exhausted the stories of our lives.

Denis Kuny came to see us, during the first few days. He had been granted a visit to discuss the question of an appeal. What he had to say, in fact, was that there would be no appeal for most of us, and for none of the women, as our sentences were more or less what he'd expected, and there was a chance that the appeal court would increase them. We weren't disappointed, as we hadn't expected either an appeal or any reduction of sentence. I thought I'd better tell him I'd assaulted a police officer. "Denis," I said. "I hit Schroeder." He seemed to want to prepare my defence from the beginning, and replied instantly, "No you didn't," but I answered, "I did. Dozens of people in the court must have seen me." He sighed at the possibility of yet more trouble ahead, but there was nothing to be done unless I was charged.

We were delighted to see him and talk to him; it was a diversion from life as sentenced prisoners, which we had already begun to find oppressively monotonous. He is usually charming and lively, but that day he seemed distressed, and very subdued. We all kissed him on the cheek, in turn, to say goodbye, and it was like kissing a statue. I dare say we looked more woebegone than we knew, and pathetic, in those khaki dresses.

Sylvia was taken away a few days later. She was told to pack her things, and that was the last we saw of her till near the end of the year. We heard later, from a visitor, that she was on trial again, this time near Port Elizabeth.

In the course of arrests and interrogations, the police were collecting new evidence all the time, and they quite often used this evidence against people already convicted on political charges, taking them from prison to court, and getting them further sentences. The effect on the prisoners, of seeing yet more time in prison stretching ahead of them, must have been shattering, and we all dreaded that it might happen to us. The police visited some others of us, too, during our last few days at the Fort, to seek further information and to threaten further charges if they didn't get it.

Schroeder was one of the two sent to visit me. He didn't look happy, but said nothing about my blow to his wrist. In fact, the police ignored that incident, never mentioned it. That day, I found myself faced with something from three years before.

Soon after South Africa had left the Commonwealth, the Republic had been declared and the presidential office put in place, there had been a move to confer the freedom of the city of Johannesburg on the State President, CR Swart. The Congress of Democrats had put out a leaflet opposing it on the grounds of Swart's record, a number of white ratepayers – notably the Black Sash – had lobbied their councillors, and the move was defeated. Of course, we had taken legal advice on the leaflet. It had gone to two or three lawyers, including Joe Slovo, and they'd found it free of libel. They hadn't thought to consider it in the light of a brand-new law on the statute books, protecting the dignity of the State President. The leaflet was manifestly disrespectful towards CR Swart, as it was intended to be, but it had been a surprise to everyone when Piet Beyleveld as national chair of the Congress of Democrats, Ben Turok as national secretary and Eve Hall as regional secretary, were taken to court and fined.

I had been responsible for the leaflet, for, in consultation with national and regional committees, I had done the research for it, written it, taken it to the lawyers, and organised the working party that had put it in the post. The police had discovered this through Schroeder's tapes, for I had mentioned it to Sylvia in my flat. They hinted that they might refrain from prosecuting me if I gave information. I wasn't prepared to give information, but, till the end of my sentence, I was afraid they'd bring the charge against me. I wasn't sure whether or not I'd simply be fined, as the others had been, and longed to be reassured that I wasn't in danger of getting an extra spell in gaol, but Denis had paid his visit and, after that, there was no lawyer to advise me. When I asked to see a lawyer, the prison authorities said I might see one only if and when I had actually been charged.

Two weeks after being sentenced, we were moved to Barberton Prison.

CHAPTER 8

Serving a sentence

Pixie's and Mollie's tales of long-term gaols had created visions in our minds of the civilised places sentenced prisoners were sent to, and we wanted to be moved, as soon as possible, to where we could settle down. The Fort was not designed as a long-term prison, and there was nothing there to keep us occupied, no real work to do. We had registered for correspondence courses with the University of South Africa, and the academic year was well advanced by then, but we were told we couldn't have our study material until we'd been moved to the gaol where we were to spend our sentences.

At last, the day came. We were given our clothes after breakfast, and told to get ready. We weren't told where we were going.

Someone new was escorted in: Stephanie Kemp. She had been brought from Kroonstad very early that morning, so it became clear we weren't going there. We hadn't met her before, but, four or five months earlier, had read in the newspapers about her trial in Cape Town, and her two-year sentence. She was a physiotherapist, twenty-four years old, who had belonged to a small organisation calling itself the African Resistance Movement, that had made a protest against apartheid by carrying out sabotage on installations, like pylons. We were very pleased to see her, and she was pleased to see us, for she had been held strictly on her own since being sentenced. She had had a hard time in detention, where a detective named Van Wyk had taken her by the hair and slammed her head against the floor, to make her talk.

We travelled in a small, closed van, of a kind we'd become familiar with while being driven to and from court. In the back, where prisoners sat, there were two very small windows, and the seating consisted of two fixed, box-shaped, metal benches running down each side. There was nothing else. Surfaces were all flat metal, smooth, glistening, with nothing to hold on to. Each time the driver accelerated, or applied his brakes, we slid along the benches, and nearly always landed in heaps on the metal floor. In this way, we travelled from Johannesburg to Barberton in what was then the Eastern Transvaal. Our escort was Colonel Aucamp, who sat in front with the driver. We had our lunch at a small-town gaol on the way, locked in a cell, with prison food in metal dishes, and spoons to eat it with. I suppose Aucamp and the driver enjoyed the hospitality of the prison staff.

In the middle of the afternoon, we arrived at Barberton Prison. Admission procedures took some time. The matron and some of the assistant wardresses took our particulars and our prints, ordered us to strip naked, took away all our clothes and nearly all our other personal possessions. Our spirits sank at the manner in which they spoke to us, and at the bleakness of the place.

We put on the prison clothes we were issued with, and then, as we were ordered to do, stood in a row, holding our new prison cards, each of which bore name, prison number, date of release, and the nature of the "offence". We were then addressed by a squat, stout, spectacled man in uniform, the officer commanding the prison. His name was Pretorius, and he had the rank of brigadier. He told us this was where we were to spend our sentences. It was the end of the road.

The female prison in Barberton was quite a new building, and the section we were in was painted green and cream, concrete floored and soulless. There was a large central space, furnished with a table, chairs, a couple of cupboards, and concrete sinks. One large cell opened off it, and three tiny single cells. All cells had outer windows, and each single cell had a small window opening on to the central space. All windows were barred, of course, and, though the external windows gave plenty of light, they were set far too high in the walls for us to be able to enjoy a view from them.

There was a bathroom and a lavatory, a small, shelved store room, and a tiny room housing wood, coal, and the wood and coal stove that heated the water in the bathroom. A large courtyard, with washing lines and a patch of grass, was surrounded on two other sides by prison offices, and on the fourth side by a high wall, separating it from another courtyard in another section.

There were only two ways into the rest of the prison: the main door, with its heavy grille, from the central room into the corridor, and another, leading from the courtyard, presumably to another corridor. We never saw where the courtyard door led, for it was scarcely ever opened, and then, only for a very short time, and we were always locked up first.

That first night, I suppose it was just after five when we were locked in our cells, but we had no way of knowing the time, because we didn't have our watches. Esther, Mollie and I seemed to be thought of as the harder cases, because we were in the three single cells, with nothing to do, nothing to read, and no one to talk to. Flo, Ann and Stephanie, together in the large cell, had each other's company. They had two luxuries as well: a tap, though with no washbasin, only a drain in the floor, and a lavatory. Ann, I was later told, used the tap as a foothold, that night, to climb up and look through the window. She saw the glare of floodlights, and she heard the voice of a guard. "Ek sal jou kop skiet," he shouted, "I'll shoot your head", so she climbed down again.

When the lights were out, and my head was on the pillow, I heard, through my high window, that the night was alive with sound. Highveld nights are silent, but now I heard rustles and squeaks and chirrups, like the nocturnal sounds of my native Natal, not far away. It was the only thing that comforted me as I fell asleep.

It was just as well that we all fell asleep early, because a loud rising bell rang well before dawn. I called to Mollie through my little window, and asked her what she thought the time was, for, as a country girl, she was good at guessing it. "I don't know," she called back, "but it's bloody early."

It was five-thirty. Our doors were unlocked at six, and breakfast came soon after, with a rattle of locks, a slamming of grilles, a clatter of pots and pans, and a lot of shouting from the wardresses. After breakfast, came the work. The main door and its grille were opened for a few moments to admit some black prisoners, carrying piles of men's khaki shirts and shorts. The shirts smelt very strongly of sweat. It seemed prisoners wearing them got only one clean shirt a week, and they had been doing hard physical work in a hot climate. Some had clearly been heaving coal, for their shirts were dark with coal dust. There were canvas jackets as well, and some pairs of tough khaki shorts. Our task was washing these clothes, in cold water, in the concrete sinks, rubbing them very hard against the concrete ridges down the sinks, and hanging them to dry in the courtyard. There was nothing for us to do but get on with the job. Stephanie remarked in a low voice that the prisoners in Kroonstad used washing machines.

Nearly every week, at least one of the shirts – and usually a pair of shorts too – came in caked and stiff with dried blood over the kidneys, from floggings. There were also caked deposits of the yellow sulphur ointment that was applied after floggings. It was evidence of dreadful suffering, a sign that, while life was bad for us, it was far worse for others. I remember one morning when, faced with a shirt like this, Mollie couldn't stop crying.

Those first weeks were a shock. The wardress on duty didn't carry keys, but was locked in with us, and had to press a bell if she needed anything. The keys came in, with a second wardress, when we were about to be locked into our cells or let out of them. We weren't given knives and forks, in case we used them as weapons against the wardress, and we ate with spoons, which made it very difficult to deal with the leathery beef they dished up for us at first. The second wardress used to bring in a bread knife to cut the loaf into slices, and then immediately take it out again. We weren't allowed to have our face creams, and, once or twice, when my face felt unbearably dry, I used cooking fat.

Twice a day, soon after unlock, and just before we were locked up for the night, we had to stand on "parade". The wardress would yell, "Parade!" and we'd hurry to the central space, to stand in line, as we had for Brigadier Pretorius that first evening, one hand behind our backs, and the other holding our prison cards out for inspection. I can see some function for this ritual in a large section, where the presence of hundreds of prisoners must be checked each day against lists of names and prison numbers. There was little point to it in our section, where there were so few of us that the wardresses knew us all well by name. Later on, as we began to mislay our prison cards, or accidentally wash them in the pockets of our uniforms, it made no difference to the administrative running of the section, and eventually we stopped using them altogether.

We were treated with studied rudeness. Curt orders were shouted at us, to do this, do that, sweep a patch of floor yet again, stand in line, hang the shirts in the courtyard, not on this line, but on that line, and only in the presence of a wardress, for we weren't allowed out there on our own. The worst shock of all was that we weren't allowed to talk, not while we were washing at the sinks, nor even at meals. Conversation was allowed during exercise in the courtyard, but the wardress used to follow us, listening to every word.

We obeyed these orders, more or less. At the Fort, we had seen the sanctions that could be used against prisoners who committed what seemed to us absurdly trivial offences. The most common punishment was to be locked up for twenty-four hours without food. It was called "getting three meals". A prisoner would say, "I got three meals", when what she meant was that she'd been deprived of them. We had seen a prisoner, a good jazz singer outside, get three meals for greeting us with a short burst of song when we came back from court after the verdict. The prison authorities could impose any number of days without meals, but not consecutively, for, according to the regulations, days of starvation had to alternate with days on "spare diet" and, over longer periods, there had to be days of ordinary prison diet as well. The prisoner could be locked up in this way for as long as a year, and, like Gertie, with only a nightdress, blankets and a mattress.

None of us felt she had the strength to face that, and so we did as we were told, though the silence was the worst aspect of our lives at that time, far worse, even, than those terrible shirts. It meant that the three of us in single cells never had a conversation with anyone, neither in nor out of the cells. It was like being back in solitary. Even when I had the chance to exchange a few hasty, furtive words with someone else, I found I'd forgotten how to do it. During lock-ups, in my single cell, I used to listen with envy to the muffled sound of Flo, Ann and Stephanie chattering in the cell across the section. They had plenty to talk about, as Stephanie was new to the group, and the other two could exchange tales of their experiences with her.

We had even less communication with the outside world than with each other, since, as "D" category prisoners for the first six months, we were allowed only one visit, and only one letter in and one letter out. Our solace was study; throughout our sentences, but particularly at this time.

We had registered with the University of South Africa because comrades outside had told us to. I think the money came from friends and family in some cases, and from the Defence and Aid Fund in others. I never found out who paid for me. I had hardly anything in the bank. My family wasn't helping. They hadn't got in touch with me, and were trying to pretend to their friends that nothing had happened.

Post-graduate study wasn't allowed, so graduates and non-graduates alike registered for courses for first degrees. Our study material arrived after a week or two, and then there were notes to read through, books to order from the university library and from the bookshop, assignments to work on. There was excitement when assignments came back, marked, and with comments. We had to work hard, for it was May, and we were preparing for examinations in November.

The course notes came with lists of recommended reading, and we – or rather, our friends and families – bought the recommended books.

We began to amass a library, which was kept in the store room, and which was of benefit to all of us, for we all used it. I filled in gaps in my reading with novels belonging to those who had registered for first-year English. There was no real life worth speaking of; I had only reading, nothing else, to fulfil the need for new experience, and I have never read with such relish and delight. I began to ration myself, as I'd rationed games of patience in detention, because I was afraid I'd read everything we had within a few months, if I wasn't careful.

We all read eclectically for, apart from the novels recommended by the English department, we had between us a range of books prescribed by the history, history of art, and cultural anthropology departments as well. The prison regulations prevented my finishing my Master's thesis so I studied cultural anthropology, and discovered a new intellectual dimension. Reading Ann's books, Esther discovered, and was enraptured by, ancient Egyptian art, and conceived a longing, which she eventually satisfied in 1994, to see it for herself. Later on in our sentences, Sylvia learned from one of her books that Russian revolutionaries before 1917, when banished to Siberia, became well-read people. The same thing was happening to us.

At the beginning, it seemed there were orders from the top, that we weren't allowed to read any books not related to our course of study. It was impossible to enforce this rule with prisoners in a shared cell. It was difficult to enforce it with those in single cells, as it meant that a bored and tired wardress, eager to get us locked up and go off duty, would have had to check book lists, and names against lists of courses, twice a day. It didn't get done. This, I think, was when our conditions began to relax.

The wardresses were the first to change. They had been told we were ruthless and dangerous, so at first they were alarmed at being locked in with us. However, as time passed, and we proved not to be physically violent, alarm turned to boredom. They must have found the silence as oppressive as we did, and they began to chat. They were curious about us, and one of them even tried to find out, in a roundabout way, whether the rumour was true that we wanted to sleep with black men (for that was how many whites perceived our political position). We explained what we stood for, and refused to show we understood what she was really getting at.

They must have felt very confused in their relationship with us. They were white racists, brought up in a white racist ethos, living and working in a situation of institutionalised racial discrimination. They thought that a loud and bullying manner, a tone of rough contempt, was appropriate for dealing with the hundreds of black prisoners whose lives they ruled absolutely. But we were white, the only white prisoners in the gaol, and, though they had been told to treat us like any other prisoners, their upbringing had taught them to speak to whites as equals, in a courteous, friendly way.

One wardress, in particular, found the situation too much for her. She was a lively and intelligent young woman, was specially assigned to us from the beginning, had been given some special training in dealing with political prisoners, and had even been brought to the Fort to observe us before our sentences began. I think this assignment must have had some connection with the NCO's stripes that appeared on her arm. She had been friendly and pleasant at the Fort, so we were offended when, at Barberton, her manner changed, in accordance with the policy of the place, and she became as rude and disagreeable as the others. One day, as we stood in line, waiting to be locked up, we were driven beyond endurance; Flo (I think it was) began to tax her indignantly with the way she was speaking to us, and we all joined in. She burst into tears, and told us she couldn't bear it, because we were just ordinary women. She relaxed after that, but didn't stay much longer. It was the wardresses who cultivated the crudest and most overbearing manners who made a career for themselves there, and climbed the ladder of promotion.

They began sending in very young, very inexperienced, girls to do duty with us; new recruits to the prison service, most of them shy and somewhat in awe of us. One of them asked me once how much I'd been paid to be in the Communist Party. I laughed, and told her we'd never been paid anything, that we ourselves had done the paying. This surprised her, so I had to go to the English-Afrikaans dictionary to look up the Afrikaans for membership subscription, to explain that we'd all paid membership subscriptions, and evidence to this had been led in court. We knew what she'd been reading recently, because she'd left it next to the stove: it was a picture-story magazine, carrying a story about communists. They were murderous villains, who dressed in South African army uniforms to go and massacre villagers.

More and more, within the narrow confines of the section, we ran our work and our lives, while these young women read their picture magazines or did their knitting, occasionally gossiping or joking with us. Later on, one of them taught me to crochet. They would sit out of sight of the door into the corridor, in case the matron in charge should take them by surprise, and find them idling.

The matron was about thirty-five, good-looking, but formidably aggressive. She never significantly softened her manner towards us, and never ceased to set her staff an example of screaming and rudeness, but, it seemed, she spoke to the staff themselves like that, as well as to the prisoners. The younger wardresses (who couldn't restrain themselves from gossiping) were full of excitement when it became known that a man had invited her to go fishing with him one weekend. I think they hoped a love affair would make her better-tempered, or she might marry him and go away, but nothing came of the relationship, and it was generally believed that she must have put him off by screaming at him.

As time went on, some softening in policy filtered down from the top, and some of the worst restrictions were lifted, one by one. I started going barefoot, except at "parade", because my prison shoes were hard and uncomfortable. The shirts were replaced by jerseys to be darned, and, later on, it was warders' sheets to be washed and ironed. Soon after we began on the married warders' sheets; however, the wives of the married warders complained about the standard of our ironing, and we were demoted to the sheets of the unmarried warders, who, it seemed, weren't very fussy, and got their sheets into a terrible state. It certainly didn't seem to have occurred to the prisons to break the traditional mould of men's and women's work: women prisoners were given washing, ironing and sewing; men did woodwork, metal work and general maintenance.

When the first summer came, and it was hot in our cells, the wooden doors were left open during lock-up, and were never locked again. The heavy, locked grilles were quite enough to restrain us. We could then talk to each other from cell to cell, across the central space.

Stephanie was the first to be promoted out of "D" category. A large adjacent room was incorporated into our space; a door was knocked through, and its door into the corridor was bricked up. Stephanie was moved in there, was made a "C" prisoner, and, after serving just over a year, was given a reduction of sentence, and released. Any form of reduction of sentence for political prisoners was very rare by that time, and she was the only one among us whose sentence was reduced in any way. Aucamp must have been instrumental in this, for he had been to Barberton several times to see her alone. The rest of us made wry jokes to each other, about people who weren't communists, only saboteurs; for it seemed that, in Aucamp's eyes, and in the eyes of the apartheid regime, a saboteur was regarded as less dangerous than a communist, especially if she was a daughter of the Afrikaner people.

The new cell must originally have been designed as an office, not as a cell, because the windows were set at the height considered normal outside prison, and, later, after Stephanie had left and we'd moved in, we used to crowd in there to watch our visitors arrive and leave. We could watch, but we knew from my experience when Dinah had visited me in Pretoria, that waving or calling would bring trouble.

Over the months and the years, the rest of us were promoted to "C" and then to "B" category. We asked for, and got, the chess and Scrabble stored with our possessions. We got permission to buy tenniquoits for the courtyard, table tennis for the central room, face cream, equipment for knitting and embroidery, drawing paper and pencils. Someone's family sent in a record player. We got permission to play records for an hour each evening, after lock-up, and permission to receive presents of books and records from our visitors. We got a clock.

"B" prisoner status brought permission to buy a monthly tobacco ration. I bought loose tobacco and papers, as the tobacco went further that way. It also brought permission to buy periodicals approved by the prison authorities. I ordered the *Times Literary Supplement* for six months, but the prison censor usually cut out so much before it got to me, that I gave up buying it. In any case, I found I got little pleasure from all those book reviews, when I couldn't read the books.

Women's magazines, of the bromide sort, came through easily enough. As a result, while we knew nothing about President Johnson's policy in Vietnam, we knew all about Twiggy, the top British fashion model of the time, and even the name of her boyfriend. We knew nothing about political developments in South Africa or anywhere else, but we soon knew a lot about the fashion revolution of the sixties, the bold patterns and colours, hemlines, the changing shape of clothes. We knew all about innovations in fashion at second hand, and saw them directly only as embodied in the khaki uniforms of the younger wardresses, whose hemlines rose, but then fell again almost immediately, presumably at the orders of the matron in charge. Her own skirts remained firmly at knee length.

There were comings and goings during this time, though the group remained very small, and in the three and a half years that section was used for white women political prisoners, there were only twelve women altogether, never more than seven or eight at a time.

The first person to arrive after us was Sylvia, who was brought from Port Elizabeth with another sentence of four years, bringing her total sentence to six years. Her trial had been a terrible experience, and she was very much disturbed by it. She told us the story, mostly in whispers in the courtyard, even when secrecy didn't seem to be necessary, but she lapsed occasionally, and told us parts of the story openly, at the table, where the wardress could hear, and we knew there might be a microphone. Her troubles weren't over yet, for she had an appeal coming up, and she spent night after night trying desperately, and in vain, to remember what she had been doing on a certain day four years earlier, for she had no alibi. She knew only that the charges against her were false.

What had happened to her was not uncommon in those days. People who had given evidence for the state in one trial often went on to give evidence in others, and became what were known as "roving" or "travelling" or "professional" witnesses. Some "roving witnesses", Beyleveld, for example, and Hlapane, as they went from trial to trial, told the truth, or something close to it, but often evidence was manufactured, for there were witnesses who were desperate enough to say whatever the security police told them to say, if they could gain indemnity by it.

Sylvia was the victim of a frame-up of this kind. A former ANC activist, turned "roving witness", gave evidence at her trial. He told the court that the underground ANC had used her as an emissary, to inform the ANC in the Eastern Cape that the organisation was abandoning its policy of peaceful resistance, and turning to armed struggle. He claimed to have been present at a meeting at which she had unfolded the new plan, and he gave a date in 1961, before Umkhonto we Sizwe had been launched, when Sylvia was twenty-three years old.

Anyone who knew anything about the ANC knew it would never have considered sending a twenty-three-year-old white woman to explain so important and so delicate a matter as the new policy of armed struggle, especially to experienced, campaign-hardened veterans like the Eastern Cape leaders. Govan Mbeki was brought to the trial by helicopter from Robben Island, to give evidence that it wasn't the policy of the ANC to have members of any race other than African. Until he'd been gaoled, he'd been a leader of the ANC, both nationally and in the Eastern Cape, and certainly had the authority to speak about ANC policy, but the court favoured the state witness, and Sylvia found herself facing six years.

When the verdict was overturned, Sylvia, in Barberton, didn't hear about it till several days later, and only then from the Church of England chaplain, on his regular visit. With no newspapers, and no visits during that time, she had had no other way of finding out the result of her appeal. The prison authorities told her nothing, though they ought, surely, to have given her the information that her sentence had been so drastically reduced.

Ann was taken back to Johannesburg for further charges, for slogan-painting done some years before, and for which she was sentenced to a further six months. There was no frame-up there, for she had certainly helped to paint those slogans. Ludi gave evidence against her, and, presumably, the police hadn't charged her before because they had wanted to keep him under wraps until the big trial was over. This was before were were allowed tobacco, but she had been able to buy cigarettes in the basement of the magistrates' court, and she brought a packet of twenty Texan back to Barberton, concealed in a tin of talc powder, whose top she had removed and then replaced very carefully. The cigarettes carried a strong smell of the talc. "Ugh," we said, as we lit them after the wardresses had locked up and gone off duty, "these cigarettes taste of scent." Ann cried, indignantly, "Well, I like that, after I've gone to so much trouble for you people." We had to assure her that we enjoyed the cigarettes all the same; and we did, of course. We were in no position to be choosy.

Violet Weinberg arrived, with Leslie Schermbrucker, Ivan's wife, to serve two-year sentences, which ran on after the rest of us had been released. Both of them had been kept awake during detention, for days and nights on end, and had finally been convicted of harbouring and taking care of Bram Fischer, while he was in hiding. We heard for the first time from them that Bram had been captured, tried again, and sentenced to life imprisonment. We heard a good deal of the story.

Another guess of mine had been proved right. I can't remember whether Violet ever came to my flat while Schroeder was living next door, but it was impossible that her name should not have cropped up, innocently, in conversation from time to time, because I, and nearly everyone who visited me, knew her. Yet she was the only person, in all our intersecting social circles, whose name was not among those printed in capitals in the transcripts of Schroeder's tapes, she didn't even appear in them. The conversations recorded on those tapes were like a panoramic group photograph of everyone we knew, with a single figure cut out. I thought at the time that the security branch must have deliberately omitted all mention of her from those transcripts, and their only possible reason could have been that they were watching her carefully, and didn't want to give her an obvious warning. I hoped she was being careful, but it turned out that she wasn't being careful enough.

It was she who had told the police where they could find Bram, but no one person was altogether to blame for Bram's capture. Under unbearable duress, people had broken down all along the line.

Violet was as much of a mixture of a person as most of us. She was efficient, capable, very courageous; sometimes generous, kind-hearted and humorous, sometimes obdurate, narrow-minded and intolerant. She had thought of herself as a strong person, and had despised people she thought of as weak. Her own strength had failed, and, by her own standards, she had turned out to be weak. She couldn't forgive herself, blamed herself as severely as she would have blamed anyone else, and suffered a great deal.

Issy Heymann had sent her a message from detention. He'd got it past the policeman present at his visit, by using an old, joking name for her, a Yiddish phrase meaning, "Aunty comrade". The message said, elliptically, that she should go into hiding, because he'd told the police she knew where Bram was. Issy reproached himself so bitterly for implicating Violet and pointing the way to Bram, that, after this, in shame and despair, he tried to cut his wrists in his cell.

He behaved heroically later, when the security branch took him to give evidence in one of many small trials, which was held, I believe, in the cells below the court. If he had protected himself by testifying, it's unlikely that he would ever have suffered disgrace in the eyes of his friends and comrades outside, for they need never have known. However, he followed his conscience, and, because he believed it was wrong to give state evidence against comrades, he refused to give it. He served a year in gaol for that. The trial got little publicity, and Issy's loyalty and integrity remained unsung.

When Violet got his message, she should have taken his advice and gone into hiding. She didn't, and, when telling us about it, never gave what seemed like an adequate reason. I think she may have wanted to prove it was possible to withstand the pressures of detention, sleep deprivation and interrogation. No one could withstand them. She held out for over forty-eight hours, to give Bram time to get away, and then told the police what she knew.

Bram was told of her arrest very soon after it had taken place, so he had ample time to move out of his house. Speaking to us, Violet never addressed the question of why he hadn't done so. I think she may have been too preoccupied with her own sense of guilt to question what he had done. Many years later, after my release, I spoke to people who were able to offer some insight: notably Ralph and Minnie Sepel in London, and Bram's daughter, Ilse, in Johannesburg.

Bram had been under tremendous strain for the previous eighteen months. The Rivonia trial had placed a great burden on the defence team, for they felt a responsibility for saving the accused from the gallows. The day after sentence was passed, Molly drowned before his eyes, in spite of his frantic efforts to save her. Three months later, he was arrested. Soon after, he spent a few weeks in the United Kingdom, but, though he saw friends, it wasn't a holiday, because he was discussing his future plans, at the same time as arguing a case. Then he came to trial, and, a month or two later, he was in hiding.

In hiding. in his new identity, he was very lonely. Violet and Leslie had been visiting him, and, while following Violet, the police had seen her talking to him, but hadn't recognised him. Others began to visit him to cheer him up. In her autobiography, the writer, Mary Benson, has described her friendship with him, and her visits to Mr Black's house. Ilse was another visitor. He badly needed this contact with people he knew, but every visit created a security risk, and it had to be only a matter of time before the police caught up with him.

Perhaps he felt the hunt was all but over, perhaps sadness, stress and the after-effects of shock had caused a paralysis of the will, perhaps he was too ready to believe Violet would stand up to interrogation. Most likely, it was a combination of all three. He didn't move, though he had more than one possible exit; Mr Black even had a passport. He was still in the same house when the police came to arrest him.

The Sepels fled as soon as they got their warning. In one crowded, frantic, tumultuous day, that Minnie told me was the worst of her whole life, they drew money from the bank, applied for passports and got them, bought air tickets for themselves and their two young sons, packed their clothes, got to the airport, and boarded an evening flight to Heathrow. They were only a few hours ahead of the police, who came for them the next morning.

There were two more prisoners. Sheila, now twenty years old, came in to do six months for slogan-painting. She had been out on bail pending an appeal which she had known would fail, and she was therefore able to choose when to begin her sentence. When she was ready, she withdrew her bail and presented herself at the police station, choosing a time when she felt her mother might need to be consoled and cheered. She knew she'd almost certainly be sent to Barberton.

Diana Schoon, then the wife of Marius, came in too, at another time, also to serve a sentence for slogan-painting. She was a delight at first, charming, and full of lively jokes and gossip. She was, indeed, a delightful young woman, but highly-strung and very young, and the place began to get her down, after a while. It got us all down; Barberton Gaol had a way of bringing out the worst in everyone.

Diana started getting hysterical fits, during which she'd give a high-pitched scream, and then fall down in a faint for a few minutes. We believed this hysteria was based in the hope that it would get her out of gaol early, for we all knew about a short-term woman political prisoner, some years before, who had been released early because she couldn't stop crying. Those palmy days, however, were over, and Diana, poor girl, served her full term. The screams were nerve-shattering though, and all the more so because they were pitched very high, on the same note as the squeak of the hinges on the door into the corridor. When we oiled the hinges in the section, we used to leave that hinge alone, because the squeak was a warning that the matron in charge was coming in or, at least, looking in.

It seemed the screams were as trying for others as they were for us, for, one day, the matron flung back the grille with a crash, strode in and, with no more ado, dosed Diana with a spoonful of paraldehyde, an antiquated sedative, but, I suppose, the most modern sedative available in that gaol. It knocked her quite unconscious for twenty-four hours, providing a welcome break for everyone. When she awoke, it seemed she too had welcomed the oblivion of that day, and wanted more days like it.

Every arrival was greeted with enthusiasm, as the news they brought in gave us something fresh to talk about. Newcomers, for their part, came into a situation much easier than that which had prevailed at the beginning. For example, Violet, who was still a "D" prisoner when she arrived, benefited from our "B" prisoner status, for she was a smoker, and we unobtrusively gave her little parcels of cigarettes or tobacco before each lock-up. All the same, coming straight from other prisons, they were all shocked at the grimness, the bleakness of our lives, and, eventually, all began to be affected by the place.

Even in its better times, our regimen was harsh. In the mornings, we worked from seven till eleven. "Exercise", in the courtyard, or at the table tennis table, lasted till the arrival of midday dinner, half an hour later. After we'd eaten, and washed the dishes, it was time to be locked up, and for the wardresses to go off duty. We were unlocked again, some time between one and two, and we worked till the second "exercise" period at four. Supper came at four-thirty, and we were locked up again, just after five. Lights went out late, at ten, to give us time to study. After our doors were left open, there was no need for the night-duty wardress to come round to turn them off, for we could reach through the grilles and turn them off ourselves, when we chose. We slept until the rising bell at five-thirty.

On Fridays, we scrubbed the concrete floor of the whole section, with scrubbing brushes and blue mottled soap, put on fresh polish, and gave it a shine. Sometimes, we were told (I cannot say "asked") to remove the old polish with paraffin, before applying a fresh layer of polish. We all hated this work, so Friday mornings were difficult times, and when people quarrelled violently over some trivial matter, it was usually then. After that, we took it in turns for a bath (the rota person would have been working hard at the stove, to make plenty of hot water), put on clean uniforms, and were ready at eleven for the visit of the commanding officer, who received us in the matron's office down the corridor, for what was called "complaints and requests". We had not lost our political activists' habits, and always had a meeting beforehand, to decide what we were going to push for, and who should raise which questions with him.

Those brief walks to the office, other expeditions down the corridor to see the prison chaplains, or Colonel Aucamp, when he came, and the annual visits to the dentist (for which we paid) were the only times we ever left the section, except for once, later in our sentences, when the Brigadier, with the aid of a wardress or two, opened the grilles and escorted us on a walk on the lawn in front of the building.

That quite unexpected little stroll wasn't a pleasant experience, for the view we saw was the one we saw every day from the front cell, there was nothing to do on the lawn, and we felt uneasy in the company of the Brigadier and the wardresses. The next day, representatives from the International Committee of the Red Cross arrived to see us. Their visit must have been planned for months beforehand, but it was a surprise to us, for we hadn't been warned. They saw us individually, and someone told them about the outing on the lawn. "It's the same wherever we go," they replied, "an issue of sweets, or a walk, just before we arrive."

Friday afternoons were a time of relaxation, the best time of the week. The local Church of England chaplain came every fortnight, after the beginning of January 1966, to visit those who had put themselves down as C of E. On the other Fridays, we'd organise some activity, but in one of the big cells, out of sight of the main door, for we could sit comfortably on the beds, and wouldn't be in sight of the matron, if she opened the door. Sometimes, we read a play. Sometimes, Ann took a drawing class. Once, it was a life class, with Sheila as the model, but a senior wardress who came on this scene was deeply shocked, and ordered Sheila to get dressed again.

Weekends were particularly uninteresting, with long lock-ups. On Saturdays, we spent the brief time out of our cells washing our own clothes and bedclothes; on Sundays, we spent it in the courtyard. Over the Christmas season, we were allowed to play records all day, but the wardresses had a lot of time off, and we spent very long hours in the cells.

The time came for promotion from "B" to "A" category. With three-year sentences, Esther and I were eligible, and, when we heard from our visitors that Lewis and Norman, our counterparts in Pretoria, had been promoted, we applied for promotion ourselves. Promotions always happened like that: the Pretoria prisoners would be promoted, our visitors would bring the news, and then we'd apply.

Esther got her promotion, and was an "A" prisoner for the last few months of her sentence, but it was a hollow victory. She didn't get the radio and newspapers "A" prisoners were entitled to under the prison regulations, and, though the new status brought more letters, and visits, the visits were not the "contact" visits, the chance to kiss, cuddle, hold hands across a table, enjoyed by common-law "A" prisoners. She and Hymie – that star-crossed pair – still had to talk to each other through the perspex, when he visited her, till she was released.

The status brought her the privilege of being allowed to buy a piece of cheese at Christmas, and, over the Christmas season of 1967, she put her cheese on the table and shared it with the rest of us. It wasn't very good cheese; possibly it was the best Barberton had to offer; possibly the wardress who'd bought it had an uneducated taste in cheese; but it was the only cheese we'd had in years.

When I applied for promotion, the Brigadier set me up for a test which I had to fail. As I stood before his desk, hands behind my back, he said: "Middleton, you're applying to be an "A" prisoner. But when I look at this book in front of me," (he indicated the Complaints and Requests book, opened it and paged through it) "I see a lot of complaints and requests from you." I was already beginning to feel irritated with him, and replied that I saw nothing wrong in that, as we saw him every Friday morning for the special purpose of making complaints and requests, and there was even a special book to record them in.

He then said, "I suppose you don't like the way I run this gaol." Of course, there was only one reply I could make. I saw "A" prisoner status slipping away from me, but I didn't care much, and answered, "No." He pushed ahead, and asked, "I suppose you think you could run it better." I thought about this for a moment. I'm no administrator, but that side of the work could be delegated, and if I were in command of the place, there would certainly be no blood on the shirts. I replied, "Yes."

The following Friday, when he told me my application had been refused, I wasn't surprised.

CHAPTER 9

Barberton Prison

We introduced into our lives all the variety we could. We rotated the daily chores, such as sweeping and building the fire for hot water. Later, we got permission to rotate cells, and, every few months, had a meeting to decide where we would go – from communal to single cell, or from single to communal, each time with a new mixture of cell-mates.

We took it in turns to edit a clandestine magazine. The editor collected contributions and then copied it all out in longhand, on lined A4 paper, which was available because we used it for study assignments, and laid out the front page carefully. There were no bylines, all articles were anonymous, for then, should the prison authorities discover an issue, only one person would have to take the rap. We all contributed serious articles at some time or other. I enjoyed writing a piece of criticism about moral values displayed in South African picture magazines, for we had seen plenty of this form of literature, thanks to the wardresses. But, looking back, what I remember with the greatest pleasure are the fake advertisements, done, I believe, by Flo and Ann. They were a satirical commentary on prison ways and prison rules, their mindless absurdity, and how they shaped our life and work there. In particular, I recall one with a picture of a lavatory brush and a tin of Harpic, both luxuries we were never issued with. "Why use these", ran the caption, "when you have two hands?"

However, in spite of everything we were able to do to relieve the effects on ourselves, the monotony and isolation were deadening, as we passed our days, our months, our years, in that section.

Our face-to-face contacts were only with each other, and with the wardresses. The authorities took care that we had no opportunity whatever to speak to the prisoners who inhabited the rest of the prison, and minimal opportunity even to see them. Black prisoners brought our saucepans of food up the corridor, and left them outside the door, and only after they had gone, was the door was opened for us to fetch the food in. A very few times, presumably when no wardresses happened to be around in the corridor, a black woman opened the door, looked curiously at us through the grille, to see what sort of people we were, exchanged a silent greeting, and quickly closed the door again. On the very rare occasions when prisoners were brought in – to do the building work on the second large cell, or to bring plants into our courtyard, for example – we were locked up all the time they were there. Occasionally, we would hear women screaming hysterically in other sections; Diana was by no means the only woman to have hysterics. The sound of one woman screaming would set others off, in section after section. People lived near the edge of hysteria, in that gaol.

The only connection we felt we had with any prisoner outside our group was a tenuous link, and a sad one. We never saw nor heard her, and never knew her name, nor the circumstances of her case. She had been sentenced to death, and was held in Barberton for a week or two before being taken to Pretoria to be hanged. As one of the privileges of her status, she was allowed the diet prescribed for whites; so, three times a day, when the pots and pans arrived, we dished up a plateful for her, and gave it to a wardress, who disappeared with it, down the corridor. Three times a day, we remembered that regulation white prison meals, which we so disliked and despised, were to be a privilege for her, till the last morning of her life.

Prison, even an enlightened prison – and Barberton was not enlightened – creates a social and emotional, even a sensory, desert, that is in itself a punishment. You go nowhere, and you see the same people every day. Work yields little satisfaction. Food is, at best, uninteresting, and, at its worst, nauseating. Physical pleasures are not easy to come by. Early on, when things were worst, Mollie used to indulge in a fantasy that she had a secret cupboard in her cell, containing liquor and cigarettes, and, after we'd been locked up for the night, she'd open it, and relax with a drink and a smoke.

A few physical stimuli, or consolations, were available. Some of them were prescribed by the doctor, for we had good health care, far better than that available to the black prisoners. We all had supplies of tranquillisers; and a soothing cough mixture was once prescribed for Esther, who saved it, and gave out teaspoonfuls all round, when we were feeling particularly low. I innocently developed a habit of sniffing the brass polish, when it was my turn to go round polishing the locks and handles. Sylvia saw what I was doing, and pointed it out to me; not that I cared, because it was enjoyable. Nowadays, it's called solvent abuse. I'd never done it before, and have never felt the need to do it since.

Mollie brewed rough liquor for well over a year, before it was discovered. We had a ration of prunes, because we had complained to the doctor that we were constipated, and she levied two or three prunes a day from each of us, all rinds from a bonanza of grapefruit that once came our way, and part of our sugar ration. She kept her brew behind the bathroom door. It was based on the bush tea we were given, and, when we drank it, it looked as if we were drinking tea. It didn't taste very good, but we liked drinking it to celebrate special days, like April 12th, which was to be a day of release, July 3rd, the day most of us had been arrested, and days we believed were important anniversaries in the struggle for the freedom of mankind: July 4th, the Declaration of Independence; July 14th, the storming of the Bastille; November 7th, the day of the Bolshevik revolution; June 26th, the day the Freedom Charter had been adopted in 1956. Eventually, a wardress happened to look behind the bathroom door, and our alcohol was confiscated, with a lot of fuss.

We all thought a great deal about food, exchanged our most delicious and succulent recipes, planned what we would eat and drink when we got out. Mollie and I both had a tendency to compulsive, comfort eating. She kept hers under rigid control, and ate too little, rather than too much, but I ate a lot of dry bread, the only food there was plenty of, and put on seven or eight kilos.

When I began to control this eating, I found great difficulty in losing all the weight, and that made me more depressed. Looking in the mirror, or even thinking about how I looked, made me feel unhappy. A new uniform was introduced for white women prisoners: a straight shirt dress in peacock blue cotton, that could be worn with or without its belt. The cut was more fashionable than that of the old khaki dresses, but the colour made me look just as washed out as before.

Soon after we were taken to Barberton, I stopped menstruating. I knew this happens quite often to women prisoners, but I saw the doctor about it, all the same. He was astonished that I thought it a serious problem. "This prison is full of women who aren't menstruating," he said, and added, "Do you really want to menstruate?" It was a sensible reply. Outside prison, I had regarded menstruation as most women regard it, that is, as an unmitigated nuisance, which is why it's sometimes called "the curse". In prison, I regarded it differently; I suppose I felt it was one of the few remaining links with my sexuality.

None of us were lesbians, and we sometimes remarked to each other that, if we had been, there would have been more softness, more tenderness, and certainly more enjoyment, in our lives. Through the gossip of the wardresses, we heard of a prisoner who had got pregnant. She was a trusty, sent out each day to clean the staff quarters. On her way through the prison grounds – so the story went – she had met another trusty. We envied her, if not her pregnancy, certainly her passionate, if brief, connection with another person.

Where the experiences of everyday life are meagre, poor, and thin in quality, inner experiences like dreams or memories, or the world within a novel one is reading, take on a stronger, clearer reality than that of the external world. In detention, and at the Fort, I had slept deeply at night, and, during the day, hadn't daydreamed about the past. In Barberton, I dreamed vividly. I think most of us did.

During the dreadful, early days of our sentences, Ann had a dream that she'd been sentenced to death, and was being held in a grim, comfortless place, like a bank, with counters and bullet-proof glass. It had been a very strong dream, and the rest of us shuddered as she told us about it. The gloom of knowing I was a prisoner underlay all my dreams, whatever happened in them. I remember one in which I was walking with Mollie, across the open veld, towards some picnic spot, and somehow, even then, I knew sadly, at the back of my mind, that I was a prisoner. I once had a very clear dream about a woman lying on the floor, sobbing and tossing in despair, and it wasn't till the afternoon of the next day that the realisation came to me that that woman was myself. Towards the end of my sentence, I began to have dreams in which I searched in vain for something, I didn't know what, along endless, badly lit corridors, and once or twice along a stretch of the street I grew up in, in Durban; not the stretch I knew best, but a particularly featureless one.

During lock-ups, memories came back to me, so intense, that it seemed as if I were involuntarily re-living those experiences, and I spent months on end going through my happier and better times. While remembering, I would sit for hours, staring at the wall, and this was a manifestation of the dreaded depression that overtakes prisoners in the middle of their sentences. I became aware that the only times I didn't feel actively, painfully, low-spirited, the only times I forgot my situation, was when I was writing an anthropology assignment, or playing chess.

Prisoners feel anger and aggression, as well as depression and inertia. In that gaol, there was a prisoner, isolated for punishment, who, one day, emptied the contents of her sanitary bucket over the head of the senior wardress who unlocked her. We heard about it from the wardress herself, who unlocked us late, because she'd had to go back to the staff quarters to have a shower and change her clothes. I knew how that prisoner felt. Now, when I read in the press about prisoners who attack the warders, smash up whatever can be smashed in the prison, break out on to the roof and sit there for days, I know exactly how those prisoners must feel. They know that retribution is certain and will be painful, but the release of suppressed feelings must seem to them to be worth it.

We didn't make any of these overt demonstrations, so I suppose it was inevitable we should turn our misery and rage on each other. There is no doubt that we supported and saved each other, and that without each other we would all have been lost, but our relationships very nearly destroyed us, too. We had no relief from each other, so anger built up, and, because we were so few, we turned it on the same individuals over and over again. We were often downright bitchy to each other, but we remained vulnerable to the extent that other people's bitchiness hurt our feelings, made us unhappy, and caused an urge to retaliate, so bitchiness bred bitchiness. We wanted kindness and friendliness, but couldn't achieve it. It was like a very unhappy marriage that those concerned couldn't escape from, except that six or eight people were trapped in the situation, instead of two, and there was no company from outside the relationship, to provide relief.

Some said they felt we showed our "real selves" in prison. I never agreed with that. I thought our real selves were what we were outside, in the real world, and that we were now all responding, in our own ways, to a narrowly specific situation. Spontaneous smiles, spontaneous laughter, were rare, and we all lost what sparkle we'd had outside, even Flo and Ann, who had sparkled the most. Natural aggressiveness – which we all possessed to some extent, and which had made us political fighters outside – became a disadvantage. Our language was peppered with four-letter words; I think using them helped defuse the aggression.

On one occasion when I was taken out to the dentist, I was struck by how pleasantly people spoke to each other, how they smiled, outside. Back in the gaol, as the grilles behind me slammed to, and the door into our section was opened to let me in, the first person I saw across the expanse of concrete floor was Mollie at one of the sinks;

silent, grim-faced and wretchedly unhappy. Near her, standing by the cupboards, was a silent, unsmiling wardress. Nothing unusual was going on. Grimness had become a way of life, and we had grown used to it.

For some of us, our studies were the source of quite tough competition, over whose main subject was the most interesting, the most socially useful, the most academically difficult and demanding. Some were intensely competitive. Some withdrew into themselves, some conceived a hatred for someone else, some patronised others. Some sought a special friend within the group, and it was interesting that the rest of the group generally discouraged this as divisive, thereby recognising that the cohesiveness of the group was valuable. Most of us did, or were, most of those things at different times. In the depths of their misery, two people once applied to the prison authorities to be separated from the others and transferred to another prison; but they didn't get their wish.

We were possessed by unreasonable irritability with each other's ways and habits. I've heard this is common among prisoners. The pettiness was extreme. For instance, I found it hard to contain myself when people pronounced the word "ate" as "eight" instead of "et", or the word "mayor" with two syllables, to rhyme with "layer" or "player". When I could no longer contain myself, the remark I made was, of course, bitchy or, at best, snide.

It's difficult for me to say what it was about me that irritated others. Leslie once told me that I was too proud to accept favours, and that, if someone offered to do something for me, I always replied, ungraciously, that I'd do it myself. I know one thing that irritated Sheila. After lock-up, I sometimes played Scrabble solitaire, and if at the first draw I drew a hand I couldn't see much future in, I would throw the tiles back with a clatter, and start again. I remember Sheila once, shouting indignantly: "Jean, you're cheating at Scrabble patience. I can *hear* you cheating."

There was also a kind of general paranoia among the malice. Wrongs and slights were imagined as often as they were real. We learned a lot about how to have our differences out, and resolve them, as we walked in twos and threes round the courtyard during exercise. But a certain aridity of the spirit set in. Even when we wanted to, we showed each other very little real warmth; and no one had much sympathy left over to be of consolation to anyone else in her problems.

The few other forms of life sharing that place of brick and concrete became important to us, in one way or another. Nasturtiums grew in a bed round the grass patch in the courtyard, and they flowered profusely in that climate. In an effort to make the place more pleasant, and to soften our lives, Mollie, Ann and Sylvia used to pick them, and arrange them in glass jars for the table, and for each cell. The sounds of the lowveld night, which had made me feel at home when we first arrived, were, of course, the sounds of small creatures, and insects. There were quite a few of them, and the insects were a nuisance.

Each spring, the warmer weather brought mosquitoes, whining and stinging, night after night, and deterred only by the gusty winds that sometimes rise in that part of the country, in spring. There were so many, it seemed unlikely that the prison authorities were taking even the most elementary precautions against their breeding in the environs of the gaol. It was useless to chase and swat them, for there were always more coming in through the windows and, in that climate, the atmosphere of the section, large as it was, would have been suffocating with windows and courtyard door closed all night. Our only protection was an ineffective brand of insect repellent we were allowed to buy in our monthly order from the chemist. The prison authorities assured us there was no danger of malaria in that area, but that isn't true now, and I suspect it wasn't true then either.

Malaria or no, the discomfort was intense and sleep was difficult. After I'd put out my light, I used to wrap myself from head to toe in my top sheet, like a tight parcel, but, at the end of the operation, I often found a mosquito inside the parcel with me, and had to unwrap myself and start again. Flo said the sight of her cell-mates on their beds, twitching and slapping themselves, reminded her of a film she'd once seen about Devil's Island.

Sometimes, flying-ants arrived in the hot early evenings. When they swarm, these creatures are attracted by light; they fly through windows, drop their wings at once and then crawl about, dying, so that the floor and furniture is covered with flying-ants, over an inch long, and discarded wings, over two inches long. There were toads that came out of the courtyard drains then, and through the grilles, hopping everywhere after the flying-ants. I remember a toad who must have been on its first hunting foray, for it was so small that one flying-ant was all it could manage, and it could barely get it down. The presence of the toads with us in our cells added to the stress already brought on by the presence of the flying-ants, but there was nothing we could do to prevent either invasion, for it was far too hot to close the windows and, locked behind our individual grilles, we couldn't close the courtyard door. One morning, Esther screamed because, when she tried to put her foot into a shoe, she found a toad already there, asleep.

Whoever swept up the dead flying-ants and their wings the next day would call me to remove gorged and sleeping toads from dark corners and behind doors, and put them back in the courtyard, for I was the only one who really liked them. They were gentle creatures, and beautifully marked: cream-coloured, speckled with brown, and with a dark brown leaf-shape on their backs.

One reads of prisoners who make friends with mice and spiders. There were other creatures, more generally popular than insects and toads. A tortoise, brought in by a wardress, lived in the courtyard for a long time; Sylvia was particularly fond of it, and named it Arnold, though we didn't know how to determine its sex, and sometimes called it Arnolda. There was a small chameleon we called Hegel, who arrived accidentally, clinging to some young nasturtium plants. I loved him. He was very friendly, and we sometimes took him into our cells during lock-up, but mostly we left him in the courtyard, and, as soon as we were unlocked, hurried out to find him. From one of the cells, in the early morning before unlock, we could sometimes see him on the grass, hunting insects with his long, lightning-swift tongue. He left as he had come: one day, we were locked up without warning, our nasturtium plants were removed, and when we went out into the courtyard, they had gone, and so had Hegel.

Not all these relationships brought us pleasure. Some were painful. There were two large chameleons that slowly died, and we didn't know why. There was a prison cat, who used to come through the grille to visit us. We all contributed from our rations to feed her, and were overjoyed when she put on weight, and then had kittens in Violet's cell, but the kittens died, one by one, evidently from some congenital defect, for, so the wardresses told us, our cat used to mate with her own son, who was the only tom cat around. Ann was even more deeply affected by these deaths than the rest of us: "Everything dies in this place," she once cried, in bitter distress, and years later, in London, when she acquired a lively young dog, she sometimes feared he might die.

In this situation, contact with life, with people outside, became very valuable indeed. We looked forward to visits and letters, in spite of the constraints on them.

Writing letters was difficult, because the things we would naturally tell our friends about, like our surroundings, the mosquitoes, the wardresses, and our fellow-prisoners, were forbidden. I was reduced to topics like the gusts of wind in spring, or the heat in summer, the nasturtiums, Arnold, Hegel, the cat and her kittens. I sometimes wrote about my studies, or a novel I'd read, but letters were limited to four hundred words, and this prevented much depth of analysis. For a while, even after they first visited me, I think Elena and Lucy suspected my brain was softening. In 1996, when Esther went through her papers, she threw away most of her old prison letters, which her family had kept. She said they were "embarrassing".

Incoming letters were, of course, a cause for excitement. Some friends confined themselves to enquiring about our well-being and our needs, because they had scruples about telling us about what they were doing, when our lives were so dull, and might seem even more dull by contrast. We were grateful for these letters, but the ones that delighted us most were about things going on outside, that we could enjoy vicariously: plays, films, restaurants, dinner parties with other friends, gossip. My former colleague, Wolfie, by then teaching in Durban, wrote wonderfully interesting letters about restaurants in Point Road, and his experiences in the classroom. Politics could not, of course, be mentioned. We read letters aloud, or at least extracts from them, at the supper-table.

I was allowed one "special" letter, that is, one outside my ration. It was from my mother's eldest brother, a farmer in the Eastern Cape, and an exploiter of prison labour. He could correctly have been described as a racist and a fascist. I think he wrote to me as a kindness, and he tried to point out to me the error of my ways. He said he'd read in the paper that when we'd painted a slogan, I had stood a little way away; he felt I had been distancing myself, and this showed that I was not beyond redemption. When I read his letter at the supper-table, we didn't know whether to laugh or be angry. It seemed that all the prison staff had read the letter, too, before it got to me, and that even they were more sophisticated than Uncle Bob, for he seemed to be a general joke. I wrote back, explaining that I had at all times regarded myself as part of slogan-painting operations, and that when I had stood a little way away, it was because I had been on guard. When his next letter came, the prison authorities offered it to me as part of my ration of letters, but gave me a choice, and I chose a letter from Philippa.

Visits took place in two rooms down the corridor, opposite the matron's office. The visitor was in one room, the prisoner in the other, and they spoke to each other through a small perspex window, perforated to let the sound through. Both prisoner and visitor stood, for, even if there had been chairs, and there weren't, they wouldn't have been able to see each other if they had been sitting down. Conversation was supposed to be confined to family and business matters, and the officer in charge of the visit had the authority to end it at once if visitors tried to tell us some of the things we wanted to know, like who was on trial, who had been imprisoned, and so on.

A code developed, but it wasn't always satisfactory: "Janey's father has gone away", a visitor might say, and the prisoner would return to the others, eager to relay all the news, but trying to remember who Janey was (she might well be a very young child) and puzzling over whether "gone away" meant being in prison, being on the run, or having escaped across the border. Philippa was good at giving this kind of information, because visiting Norman gave her practice, and she planned it carefully. She managed to get across to me news of the trial of Herman Toivo Ja Toivo of Namibia, and the impressive statement he had made to the court.

Among the highlights, were the visits of the rabbi, who came from Johannesburg twice a year, before Pesach and Rosh Hashanah. We all loved him, though only Esther and Violet, and Sheila, while she was there, ever saw him. They were radiant when they came back from these visits. They had chatted across a table, freely, in Yiddish, which the wardress on duty couldn't understand; he had given them news of their families, and told them witty, wry, Jewish jokes, which they recounted to the rest of us. He brought delicacies for the feast days, and, because he knew Esther and Violet would never keep this fare to themselves, but would share it, he brought enough for everyone, with a little extra for the commanding officer, to put him in a good temper.

Our experience with the Church of England chaplain was different. He was a local vicar, who, it seemed, didn't follow politics, and was evidently unaccustomed to the work of prison chaplain. On his first visit, he offered to take our confessions, if we had "bad consciences". He meant well, of course, and was quite shocked when we told him we didn't have bad consciences about the activities that had got us into gaol. Light began, momentarily, to dawn, and he asked, "Are you detainees?" but, when we answered, "No. We used to be detainees, but now we're convicted prisoners," he was puzzled. On his second visit, months later, he told us he had been in touch with Father Mark Nye, the Anglican prison chaplain in Pretoria, and, after that, he seemed to know a little more about how to regard us.

He couldn't have been described as sympathetic though. He avoided any kind of personal relationship with us, and, except when he brought Sylvia news of the result of her appeal, he was more comfortable with the impersonal. What he said to us during his visits sounded like his sermon from the previous Sunday, and probably was. The only secular news I remember his giving us, apart from Sylvia's, was about the flood in Florence that had devastated the Uffizzi Gallery, and the Aberfan disaster in Wales. He never told us jokes.

He was very obliging about lending me one or two books of biblical commentary, and this gave me the idea of trying to engage him in philosophical or moral disputation. I thought it would make his visits more lively and interesting, but it was a sad failure. I asked him once what he thought of a report I'd read in a magazine, about a new Transvaal Education Department ordinance that forbade any schoolgirl who had got pregnant ever to be admitted to a Transvaal school again. He replied he thought it a good idea, since it would serve as an example to the others, and I couldn't conceal my outrage. We disagreed again when I displeased him by saying I thought St Stephen was thinking as a Jew, not as a Christian, when he condemned what he believed was the wickedness of the Temple. My argument was that Stephen meant the Temple was a graven image, and I meant it very seriously, having read the chapter carefully, and given it thought.

Leslie said I should treat the chaplain "more reverently" and, though I found her argument very unimpressive, I could easily see that my hope of enjoying interesting discussions was vain. In the end, I sometimes lay on my bed, on Friday afternoons, reading, instead of attending his visits, and sent a message with the others to say I wasn't feeling well.

It's often said that prisoners' spirits begin to improve after they have served half their sentences. This is not a myth. The halfway mark is an important psychological milestone. I have described things at their worst, but, after a year and a half, or two years, we began to feel better. It showed in my metabolism; I began to menstruate again, and, towards the end, lost the extra weight, and more, without even trying. A tentative kindness, and even affection, began to show itself in our relationships, and long-standing feuds began coming to an end. And by this time, as we were getting more letters and visits, we saw more of the outside world, even if only through the eyes of others, and had more to talk about. When I wrote to Lucy: "Only sixteen more months, now, and I'll be out," I was quite serious, but she must have thought I'd gone crazy.

Towards the end of my sentence, the Brigadier asked me if I had been "rehabilitated". During the weekly interviews in the office down the corridor, he often told us that he was "rehabilitating" prisoners, and I was never sure whether these pious claims were signs of breathtaking hypocrisy, or of crass stupidity, for he seemed capable of both. At first, I didn't reply to his question, because I had no idea what he meant by "rehabilitation" in my case. He explained: "Have you changed your ideas?" I realised, with astonishment, that he meant my politics; that, in his mind, "rehabilitation" meant learning to go along with, to accept, a system of repression, of minority rule and minority privilege, cruelly imposed. I said, "No, of course I haven't changed my ideas. You've shown me nothing to change them."

The experience of prison confirmed my conviction that South African society was iniquitous, and that it, and not my ideas, urgently needed to change. I saw Barberton Prison as a microcosm of that society, where black and white were locked into a system of disadvantage and privilege, where extreme callousness was the rule, and human beings were of no account, where brutality and deprivation were used to intimidate and destroy.

The kind of work prisoners were given in gaol was designed to have a destructive effect on them. It was demoralising because it was tedious and pointless, usually required the minimum of skills, and was usually made unnecessarily difficult. It is typified in my mind by something I saw on my first morning at the Fort, when I looked through my cell window on to a wide gravel path, where prisoners and wardresses passed continually up and down. There were black manhole covers set in the path, and a prisoner, with blacklead and cloth, was keeping them shiny and black. Each time someone trod a sandy footprint on a manhole cover, she bent down and blacked it again. That, it seemed, was her job.

While we were washing by hand in Barberton, the white men political prisoners in Pretoria were sewing mailbags by hand, and Nelson Mandela, Mac Maharaj, and others, were ruining their eyes, hacking out the quarry on the Island. Other former prisoners on the Island describe how they were made to shift wheelbarrows full of gravel all day, at top speed. The purpose of imposing such labour-intensive work is clearly punitive, for all these jobs are better done by machine.

At the end of 1982, nearly fifteen years after most of us had left Barberton, prisoners there were getting the wheelbarrow treatment. Of a work party working on a dam, three prisoners died, and others were made seriously ill, through being forced to push wheelbarrows full of gravel uphill, in the full sun, and in a temperature of thirty-five degrees. When they asked for water it was refused them. When they flagged, and even when they collapsed, the warders beat them with rubber truncheons. The warders were charged, and the evidence led in court threw light on abuses in South African gaols.

The Barberton prison authorities had flagrantly broken at least one of the prison regulations concerning prisoners' health, for these prisoners had arrived at the gaol the previous night, and had not yet had the medical examination that prison regulations lay down should take place on arrival, and which, in practice, takes place at the time of the doctor's visit the next morning. One of the men who died had been having an asthma attack. It was clear the intention had been to "break" these prisoners. Later, when thirty-four of them agreed to give evidence against the warders, they were offered inducements to refuse; and then further attempts were made to "break" them by threats and intimidation. Once in court, they said they feared for their lives; they asked to be moved to another gaol, and to be held together in one cell, for safety's sake.

That was still in the future.

Before we were taken to Barberton Prison, I don't think any of us had ever heard of the place. I certainly hadn't. Visitors who came from Johannesburg during our first weeks didn't know about it either; and they thought it charming. News about prisons and prison conditions was a kind of folklore, in those days, picked up piecemeal by prisoners and their friends and relatives, passed on by word of mouth, sometimes imparted in letters. We had never seen the name of Barberton Prison in print, that we could remember, nor had we heard it, for our information came from political prisoners and former political prisoners, and ours was the first group of political prisoners to be sent there. We didn't know that black common-law prisoners dreaded its name.

We were never subjected to physical brutality ourselves while we were there, but we couldn't help being aware of its shadow, hanging over the place. Cruelty and suffering were part of life there, and it wasn't only the blood-encrusted clothes that showed it.

When new plants were brought into the courtyard, we were shut away, the courtyard door was opened, and black women prisoners brought the plants through. They were running. Through a cell window, we saw how the wardresses used the leather thongs attached to their keys as whips, to keep those women moving. They looked as if they were running as fast as they could, but the wardresses whipped them to make them run faster, and, if a prisoner had a baby on her back, it was the baby who was whipped.

A wardress told us once about a woman who had spent a year in solitary, for some prison offence, picking sisal with bleeding fingers. The sisal was used to inflict suffering in more ways than one, for, while some prisoners were picking the fibres, others had to cultivate it. The rabbi told Esther and Violet that the Brigadier had boasted to him about his practice of "breaking" prisoners in the heat and toil of the sisal fields.

The worst incident concerned a shot we heard one morning, ringing out from the direction of those fields. That afternoon, the wardress on duty, one of the very young ones, told us that a prisoner had been shot dead. The staff must have been briefed during the lunch break, for she had the story straight. "It's all right," she said, "we're going to say he was trying to escape." I'm sure she was too naive to know how much she'd revealed in these words, nor how we would feel about it. Perhaps she thought we'd be glad to hear that the honour of the gaol was going to be upheld.

CHAPTER 10

_____

Political prisoners

There are a few ways in which political prisoners are better off than those convicted of common-law offences. For one thing, they feel pride, not shame, at what they have done. In most cases, friends or families, or both, share this feeling, and are happy to give what support and encouragement they are able to. In this way, our group was fortunate – more fortunate, even, than many white prisoners, more fortunate, certainly, than the often pathetic prostitutes, petty thieves and vagrants we'd known in the Fort.

There's another side to it, though. Political prisoners may be held in extremely uncomfortable prison conditions. Partly, this is for greater security, since it's assumed, rightly or wrongly, that they have supporters outside, who are prepared to organise escapes. Partly, it's because a repressive government will do everything in its power to break the spirit of those who oppose it, to neutralise them, to cut them off from their constituencies, to prevent their giving trouble in the future. Within the prisons, the unapologetic behaviour of political prisoners can evoke a vindictive response from people in authority, and they may therefore be victimised as individuals, too.

The prison authorities in Barberton used to deny that we were political prisoners. They denied that there were any political prisoners in South Africa. This was in line with the policy of the Department of Prisons, as it was then called, which used to claim that all prisoners in South Africa had been imprisoned, equally, because they had broken the law of the land. When challenged about this, the commanding officer, matron in charge and senior wardresses fell back to the position that, though we weren't political prisoners, we were *"staatsoortreders"*, state offenders. They knew as well as we did that our section in their gaol was one of the centres that had been set up especially for political prisoners, state offenders, whatever the name. They knew even better than we did that we were not held under the same conditions as common-law offenders.

In the early sixties, political prisoners had been held together with common-law prisoners. Men had been held in prisons like Modder Bee and Leeuwkop, and it was during this period that Mollie, Pixie and others had served their six months in Nylstroom and Pietersburg. A year or two later, as numbers rose and the body of repressive legislation grew, the Prisons Department set aside certain prisons, or large sections of prisons, for those who were sentenced for opposing the government. A huge concentration of black men was being gathered on Robben Island, and a sizeable group of white men in Pretoria; there was a section for black women in Nelspruit, and the one for white women was the one we were in, nearby, and under the same command. This was how our group came to be in a maximum security gaol, though our ignorance of lock-picking had caused derision among burglars we'd met in the Fort. Tessa would have smiled, had she known.

These centres, and the prisoners in them, were supervised by Colonel Aucamp, who had nothing to do with common-law prisoners. He travelled all over the country, visiting Nelspruit, Barberton, Pretoria and the Island. It seemed he was responsible for explaining policy on the treatment of political prisoners to local commanding officers, and it was he who had given a talk to the wardresses in Barberton, about how dangerous we were. He held his own "complaints and requests" sessions with individual prisoners, and, if he felt they were weakening, might tempt them with the prospect of early release, on condition that they repudiated the political stand they had taken in the past, or gave information or confirmed information given by other prisoners, or agreed to give state evidence in political trials. He must have been in charge of the security of political prisoners too, for, from what I've heard, he was always in command of the operation, when they were moved from place to place.

In Barberton, he was consulted on what could be sent in to us from outside, and what we could send out. One of my anthropology assignments was about centralised and decentralised systems in African societies, but, because it had to be entitled *Political Organisation*, it wasn't posted off to the University of South Africa till he had visited Barberton and given his decision. There was a prescribed work about African separatist churches, called *Black Prophets in South Africa*, that I wasn't allowed to have, until he'd seen it.

Once political prisoners had been isolated from the rest, it became easy to hold them under different conditions. In Barberton, we asked repeatedly for a copy of the prison regulations, but never got one. Instead, we were eventually given a derisory little document, consisting of a few typed pages, which we were told were extracts from those regulations that affected us, and contained all we needed to know. It was plain that the commanding officer didn't want us to see what the regulations prescribed, because so many were being broken, but, within the prison, his word was law, and there was no appeal against it, except to Colonel Aucamp, from whom we were unlikely to get much support.

Political prisoners were certainly held under different conditions, and different regulations. Some differences were obvious. To begin with, political prisoners were never eligible for remission or parole (I remember reading in some official document that we shared this distinction with drug offenders and cattle thieves) or for amnesties that affected other prisoners. We all began as "D" prisoners, though common-law prisoners generally started as "C" prisoners, and were demoted to "D" category only for some serious prison offence, like violence against a warder, or an attempted escape. This was part of the effort to break our spirit. So was the fact that all political prisoners were given a hard time at the beginning of their sentences. Some were kept in solitary for six months, so perhaps we got off lightly, with the shirts, the single cells, and the ban on talking.

We knew, or rather Mollie knew, from her time in other gaols, that there were regulations allowing for newspapers and radio for "A" and "B" prisoners, and "contact visits" for "A" prisoners, which were being broken in our case. There was nothing we could do about it. In the sixties, political prisoners got few of these "privileges", as they were called. None of us saw a newspaper, heard a radio, or touched a visitor all the time we were in Barberton.

One matter in which I believe political prisoners had an advantage was that of medical attention. The authorities dared not neglect the health of prisoners who commanded a lobby outside, and were articulate, and able to tell the tale when they were released.

Where our group was concerned, the privilege was compounded by the fact that we had a little money, and could afford to have our teeth filled, whereas prisoners without money were obliged to endure progressive dental decay until the time came for the tooth to be taken out, at the expense of the prisons (I believe that this is no longer the case). One of the International Red Cross representatives told us about a prisoner he had encountered on Robben Island, who had a perfect set of teeth, except for one, which had a spot of decay. The prisoner had no money, and the Red Cross inspector had paid for the necessary treatment out of his own pocket.

The privilege was compounded by the fact of our being white. The medical care given to white prisoners was incomparably better than that given to blacks, as anyone can testify who has seen the queues of black prisoners waiting, ready stripped for the doctor, every morning, summer and winter, in South African prisons. The medical care we got at Barberton was better than that given to any black prisoners anywhere. One or two of us even had minor surgery, but without after-care, for we were hurried back from the hospital to the gaol while we were still coming round from the anaesthetic.

This was all general policy, but, within that framework, much of what we got, or didn't get, permission for seemed to be at the whim of the Brigadier. He was a coarse and intransigent person, and his decisions, which often seemed mindless and arbitrary, were, I think, usually calculated to demoralise us.

One decision concerned musical instruments, to which "A" and "B" prisoners were entitled. It was said that, years before, Norbert Erlie, the famous embezzler, had had his piano in gaol with him. Later, in the eighties, the MK man, James Mange, started a band on Robben Island, and he was a band leader when he was released in 1991. However, when Ann and I became "B" prisoners, and asked permission to get our recorders in, with sheet music, the commander refused. He said he'd never heard of women prisoners having musical instruments.

The regulations also allowed for film shows for "A" and "B" prisoners. There were film shows on the Island at that time − former prisoners there recall government propaganda films, and Westerns, that they were contemptuous of − but no films at all in Barberton, and, in our section at least, no facilities whatever for showing them.

Part of the policy was to isolate political prisoners from the outside world, and from family and friends, hundreds of miles away. This was meant to serve two purposes: to preserve tighter security, and to bring down the prisoners' morale.

Robben Island is a long way from any city except Cape Town. There must have been hundreds of wives, girlfriends, parents, in the Transvaal, Natal, or the northern and eastern Cape, who never once had the return fare to visit that prison. They were unlikely to have money to spare to send to the prisoner, who would therefore be unable to buy such small comforts the regulations allowed. Barberton and Nelspruit are a long way from even the nearest cities, Johannesburg and Pretoria. In the early seventies, a group of concerned people from Johannesburg went to see the Nelspruit women, and found that some of them had had no visitors for two years, and had no money of their own either. I heard that, after the last of our group were released, they were moved to Barberton, into the section we had occupied.

Our group in Barberton was more fortunate. Our families and friends were better off, and, thanks to them and to other well-wishers, we always had a little money: enough for such needs as study fees, books, postage for the university library books, and dental treatment, and were never short of our quota of letters and visits.

It wasn't easy for my visitors, all the same, though they had cars, and though Lucy and Elena, Wolfie and Philippa took it in turns to come to see me. They worked all week, so came on Saturdays, and it took them the whole day, starting early, to travel from Johannesburg, or from Durban, get to the prison, pay the visit, and get home again. It was enough to stretch loyalty. When I was a "B" prisoner, and allowed one half-hour visit a month, I asked for, and got, a one-hour visit every two months, and most of us combined visits in this way.

Esther suggested it to Hymie, but he refused. He was banned, and had to have the magistrate's permission to leave the district of Johannesburg, and, each time the prison regulations allowed him a visit, he made his application, and set off for the day. He once added up the number of miles he'd done, and wrote to Esther that he'd travelled the equivalent of halfway round the world, to visit the girl he loved.

Once, we were told to stand on "parade" to see a judge. He was on circuit, and, only that morning, had given the death sentence to the woman who was to share our food. He came in smiling and apparently untroubled, somewhat red in the face, and looking as if he'd enjoyed a good lunch. He exchanged greetings with us, and was ushered out again at once. It was as if the matron in charge had shown him an exhibit. That was the only time we had any kind of official visitor, apart from the security police, who visited us a few times towards the end of our sentences.

The commanding officer of Barberton and Nelspruit prisons – the jobs were combined – could do more or less as he liked, because there was no supervision, no check, on him. In those prisons, women political prisoners were isolated from most of those who made it their business to visit prisoners. The International Committee of the Red Cross went everywhere: they came to see us once, and meticulously spoke to each of us in turn. We were far from the seats of government though, and it was a long journey for busy political lawyers and MPs who visited Pretoria and the Island. They never came to the north-east. Helen Suzman, then an MP who visited prisoners, says she was told we didn't need her.

No doubt the reasons behind this were concerned partly with logistics, but I think there was another reason too: a general belief outside that women political prisoners were having a comparatively easy time of it.

Perhaps this belief had its origins in the fact that the Fischer trial women had not been kept awake by their interrogators, though both Violet and Leslie had suffered that treatment. Perhaps it existed because, on paper, the regulations appeared more relaxed for women; they allowed bedsteads for white women, for example, though the quality of the mattresses went unspecified. Perhaps people outside believed that the prison authorities treated women chivalrously. (Goodness knows, nothing less chivalrous than the Brigadier could possibly be imagined.) Some visitors were misled by the scenic charm of the Eastern Transvaal, and told us we were fortunate to be serving our sentences among those beautiful green hills. This annoyed us, because, locked behind those walls, you don't see wide, panoramic views of the scenery. In our section, we could see a hill or two from only two windows, and those narrow views soon lost their freshness and appeal.

Perhaps the misconception was based on conditions of the past, for, a few years earlier, life for the white women politicals in long-term prisons had been a lot easier than life for the black political men in Modder Bee. However, though times had changed, the notion remained, that men were at the cutting edge of imprisonment, and women inhabited some more ladylike and comfortable world.

Violet and Leslie, both deeply concerned with the care and support of prisoners, had held this belief until they themselves went into Barberton Prison, and found conditions there worse than they'd supposed. It certainly prevailed among white men prisoners. Years later, in London, I heard a man newly released from Pretoria tell an interviewer on British television about the solidarity and fellowship political prisoners in Pretoria felt with their comrades on Robben Island. I think he'd simply forgotten that any other imprisoned comrades existed. He was exasperated when I asked him afterwards why he hadn't mentioned his comrades in Nelspruit and Barberton. "Oh," he replied, in real irritation, "you women's libbers!" Those were the bad old days in more ways than one.

Attitudes have not yet completely changed though. In 1997, I heard an SABC radio programme on former political prisoners, and it consisted entirely of three interviews, with three white men. That was all. They were interesting interviews; but they weren't representative. It seemed that the producer had chosen these men to speak for all political prisoners; and one seemed to have been chosen to speak for women, for he mentioned what he called the "general perception" of women's gaols, as being "softer".

I believe that women political prisoners suffered more hardship, not less, because the fact that they were few made it possible for prison authorities to isolate them, singly or in small groups. While we were in Barberton, we heard rumours of Dulcie September's being held on her own in Kroonstad, and, nearly twenty years later, it was possible for the prisons to keep Barbara Hogan in complete isolation in Pretoria, for many months. Isolation is the cruellest aspect of a prison sentence, and this is something prison authorities know well, for they use isolation from other prisoners as a punishment for offences committed within the gaol.

The smaller the group, the more intense is the social impoverishment of each individual prisoner. This goes for contact with the outside world, as well as for contact inside; for, unsatisfactory as prison visits and letters are, the news is shared, and the lift of spirits is communicated. News going out is important too, especially for political prisoners, who may need to tell those outside about the conditions they are being held under. This is almost impossible in letters, which may be censored, but, in face-to-face visits, close friends may use a private language to communicate more than the guarding prison officer understands. The fewer the prisoners in a group, the fewer the lines of communication with the outside, so less news gets in and less gets out. Visits from lawyers and MPs are privileged, so where these don't take place, the situation is worse.

Conditions for political prisoners in South Africa improved gradually during the seventies and eighties. This was partly because of protest within the gaols, from the prisoners themselves, but only partly, because prisoners don't have much power. The prison authorities have physical force on their side, and are always able to make prisoners' lives much more uncomfortable than prisoners can make theirs.

I am convinced that the most effective force for change in the prisons was the campaigning that went on outside. Conditions in the political gaols got a lot of publicity, not in South Africa itself, for the Prisons Act of 1959 forbade publication of information about prisons and prisoners,

118

but overseas. There is no doubt that the great anti-apartheid campaigns in Europe, North America, Australia and New Zealand, and the pressures from other African states, were a growing embarrassment to the government in Pretoria.

CHAPTER 11

Time runs out

Some prisoners are said to be afraid of the world outside and its problems, to the extent that they are reluctant to leave the protective walls of the prison. I don't think any of us felt quite like that. We were all eager to get out, though we felt some anxiety about the difficulties we knew would face us.

Violet was going to have to come to terms with the loss of her son, Mark, who died while she was in Barberton. She learned about it from Sheila, who had been granted a special visit to give her the news. She was distraught when she returned from the visit; her grief was terrible to see and hear. She applied at once to be escorted to the funeral, but, to make things worse, her application was refused. Nearly thirty years later, in 1995, I thought of her when I read that Reggie Kray, the London gangster, had been granted something she had been denied, when he was taken from Parkhurst Prison on the Isle of Wight to the funeral of his gangster brother, Ron.

When Violet was released, Eli would have more than a year of his sentence still to serve, and it was clear she was going to have to rely heavily on Sheila. For the time being, Sheila was the only Weinberg left in the family home. She was twenty-one years old by then, and she had had to undertake more than one sad responsibility after her release from prison, for it was she who found her brother dead, and she who had to travel to Pretoria, as well as to Barberton, to tell both her parents, separately, the news of their loss, and hers.

Mollie was going to need the support of her mother and brother in facing a loss of her own. She had had a visit from her husband, during which he told her he wouldn't be coming to see her again. He was suing for divorce, and, by the time she went out, he wouldn't be her husband any longer, but would be somebody else's. She bore the shock stoically, far too stoically for her own good, and, after the first few days, spoke little, far too little, about her distress.

None of the rest of us had that kind of blow to bear, but we too were going to face difficulties. We had already been "named" as members of two banned organisations: the Congress of Democrats and the Communist Party. Added to that, we knew we would certainly be served with banning and house arrest orders, for our visitors had warned us that this was happening to all political prisoners, as they were released. Finding jobs would be difficult.

I faced certain unemployment, for the standard banning orders specifically forbade teaching, or even entering the premises of an educational institution. My only other skills lay in language, and the orders forbade any activity to do with publishing. I knew I'd have to go overseas, and I wanted to go to Britain, because I'd lived there for two and a half years in the early fifties. Then, I had been a Commonwealth citizen, but South Africa had left the Commonwealth since then, and now I was an alien, and needed permission to enter the country as a political refugee. I would have to leave South Africa on a one-way exit permit, for I had no chance of a South African passport.

While waiting for my applications to go through, I was going to have to live somewhere. The security police visited me twice, to find out what my address would be, for they needed an address to put on my house arrest papers. I told them I didn't know where I'd be living. I enjoyed being unhelpful, but what I said was true, none the less, for I had no flat, and no money to pay rent. I knew Elena, Lucy, or someone, would look after me, but whose house I would stay in was something they would decide among themselves. I couldn't stay with any of my political friends, because, by then, they were all banned, or "named" as members of proscribed organisations.

Banned people were forbidden to communicate with each other, and with "named" people, though nothing forbade "named" people from communicating with banned people. Members of the same family were, of course, *de facto* exempt from this prohibition, so Esther and Hymie, in the same house, would be able to talk to each other with impunity. Even so, the Minister of Justice sent them permission to communicate with each other, in a letter that arrived about two weeks after Esther had returned home.

It was a ludicrous law, but it was nevertheless strictly enforced, and led to some ludicrous prosecutions. We'd heard of a banned person who was prosecuted for waving from the public gallery in court to another banned person in the dock, and offered the defence that she'd been arranging her hair, not waving. Knowing that, after we were released, we'd be unlikely to meet and talk again for a long time, if ever, we sewed, embroidered, knitted and crocheted mementoes for each other.

Violet's presents were by far the most useful, and took a lot of hard work to produce. As she was the eldest, and the mother of grown-up children, I suppose she felt comfortable in the role of mother to the rest of us, and she made clothes for us to wear when we were released. With a lot of consultation, she ordered patterns and fabric, and, because there was no sewing machine around, she stitched everything by hand, during lock-ups. It was a tremendous task, and she did it beautifully. It meant a lot to all of us, for, walking round the courtyard in our blue shirt dresses, which were growing old and faded, we dreamed of looking glamorous when we went out. She made me a skirt, and, more than that, she made me a dress, too. "When you get to London," she said, "people are going to ask you to dinner. You'll need something to wear."

Flo and Sylvia, with two-year sentences, were the first to go, and they were taken back to the Fort for release early in April 1967. Sylvia had been lucky, for, if the appeal court had upheld the sentence she'd got at her trial in the Eastern Cape, she would have still been in prison long after the rest of us were out. Her brother had made arrangements for her to fly to London as soon as she was released, for she had a British passport, and therefore didn't need to apply for either a British visa or an exit permit from the South African government. Flo intended to try staying in Johannesburg; as a qualified and experienced radiographer, she had a better chance of finding a job than most of us.

Ann and Mollie were next. Ann felt she would probably have to leave the country, but Mollie was deeply attached to her family and the family farm, and, though her banning order would prevent her going back to work in the bookshop, she felt she'd prefer to stay in South Africa.

This meant that I'd be likely to see Sylvia and Ann again, but I wouldn't be able to help losing touch with Flo and Mollie. Overseas, I would be out of reach of South African law, and might safely write to them, because they couldn't legally be held responsible for any letters that came to them in the post. However, any letter either of them might write to me could, if the police intercepted it, be used against them as evidence in court. As things turned out, I didn't see or speak to either of them till nearly twenty-four years later, when I returned to South Africa.

Soon after Ann and Mollie went, I wrote my third-year anthropology examinations, and my three years of study in prison came to an end. Release was imminent. There were four of us left in that section: Esther and I, with six months to go, and Violet and Leslie.

We were each able to have a cell to ourselves. It didn't feel like solitary, more like having a room of one's own because, while we were locked up, we could call from cell to cell, and we could amuse ourselves pretty well as we wished, during unlock times. Our mood by that time was contemplative, even serene. I had a few weeks alone in the cell with a tap and a lavatory, and I remember reading Hopkins' long poem, *The Wreck of the Deutschland*, there, aloud, to myself, by far the best way of reading poetry. About a month later, over the long Christmas lock-ups of 1967, I read *War and Peace* in the front cell. It was a good time, as times in gaol go.

I was busy too, making small embroidered gifts for friends outside, and I made a special one for Margery, which I intended to send her with a note explaining why I hadn't been able to visit her in Parkview. By then, it didn't matter if I told her the truth, for it was no longer a secret.

The matron had given up trying to get much work out of us, and made a show, each week, of sending in a few sheets, which we made a show of ironing. There was only one iron and one ironing-table, and we ironed in turns, very slowly, while the others – the wardress on duty, too – read or embroidered or crocheted round corners, and in the cells. When the matron came to the grille, there was always someone ironing, and the squeal of the hinges alerted others, who left what they were doing and came hurrying out, flicking dusters, and doing their best to look as if they'd been using them. She probably wasn't deceived, but as long as we refrained from flaunting our idleness she turned a blind eye to it.

None of us four had further charges brought against us. None of us had been part of the disastrous slogan-painting operation. I had escaped it, Esther had been too deep in underground work by that time to undertake that kind of activity, and, though Violet had sometimes taken part as a member of a Party unit, she and Leslie hadn't been part of the "volunteer" groups.

My other activities, those that were known to the police, had already been used as evidence in the trial, and therefore couldn't be used in any other case against me. The one exception was the president's dignity case. The police had visited me again, and threatened me with it. They wanted to know who had originally hired a certain post-office box, which had been used to receive banned literature from overseas. I wasn't sure whether or not the person they wanted was still in the country, so I lied, and said I couldn't remember, and nothing came of their threat. I later learned that she wasn't in the country any longer, and I suspect that, in any case, there was no one left in the country who could have testified that I knew who had hired the box.

I am still slightly ashamed of something that happened during that time. Someone got the idea that we should play bridge. Only Violet knew how to play, and she was willing to teach us. Violet and Esther were both enthusiastic, skilful, experienced card players. I don't know about Leslie, but I think she enjoyed playing cards. I don't enjoy it, except for patience. The time I had sat playing cards with Costa in the hotel room had been the only time in years I'd taken part in a card game, and then I'd done it only to stave off anxiety. Not only do I dislike playing cards, but I'm very bad at it; have no memory for what cards have been played or by whom; no idea of how to work out what cards other people are holding.

I imagined my own misery, trapped at card games instead of reading or sewing, and I imagined the displeasure of the others at the mistakes I would most certainly make. Now that the four of us were all getting on so well, that would have been a great pity. So I refused to learn to play bridge, and, because of my selfishness, no one could play. The others were very generous about it; no one tried too hard to persuade me, and it was never mentioned again. I still feel shame, but I still have a feeling I did the right thing.

Esther and I were due to be released on April 12th 1968, but Good Friday fell on that day, and we knew that, in accordance with prison practice, we'd be released the day before. It was the only remission of sentence we got. Colonel Aucamp and his driver called for us at the beginning of the week, and took us to Johannesburg, this time in a car, not a van, for we'd be unlikely to try to escape and go on the run three days before we'd be out anyway. The Brigadier came to see us off. He put out his hand to say goodbye to me, but I felt his action was bizarre, and put my hand behind my back.

We were dressed in our own clothes, looking like ourselves again. It was the first time I'd worn lipstick for nearly three years, and I was pleased with Violet's skirt, and a long, polo-necked sweater knitted by Leslie. I had a new handbag Ann had crocheted in black raffia. My hair was in a very rough pony tail, but I knew any shortcomings there would be rectified within a few hours of my going out, for I had asked Lucy and Elena to make an appointment for me with a hairdresser for the Thursday afternoon. I was going to have lunch on the Friday with Dinah and her husband, and Dinah was planning Wiener schnitzel.

In the Fort, Esther and I were once more issued with prison uniform, and were put together in the cell that, three years before, had held seven of us. We counted the hours. The weather broke, and the next few days were rainy and cold, but we were too happy and excited to care. The food was, as always, unpleasant, but that didn't bother us either, for we knew we would soon be eating good meals. We kept ourselves going on the bread and golden syrup that was served for supper every day.

We learned that there was a political prisoner in one of the single cells, and, when no one was looking, we slipped round the corner to talk to her through her window. We found her sitting on her little stool, her Bible on her knee, a better-behaved and more dignified prisoner than any of us had been. She told us she had been sentenced to six months for painting a slogan, and was to be sent to Barberton. She was a devout Christian, filled with righteous indignation and moral courage, but too inexperienced to know that she should have had at least one other person with her to keep watch, as she painted her slogan, or to know that the walls of Park Station, in the full glare of street lights, were too public for any but the most rash of slogan-painters. She was too inexperienced to take into account the fact that the longer she stood, breaking the law, the more likely she was to be caught, and she'd chosen a very long slogan: "Remember the United Nations Declaration of Human Rights". I think she said she'd been arrested before she'd finished. We felt a lot of respect for her sincerity.

Our banning notices had been served on us before we left Barberton. Esther had been placed under twelve-hour house arrest at her home in Yeoville. I had a breathing space from house arrest, because I had no fixed abode, but all the other restrictions were there, including a stipulation that I report to the Hospital Hill police station every day. The prohibition on communicating couldn't be enforced while Esther and I were being held together in a cell, but would come into effect as soon as we walked out through the door of the prison, and, from that moment, we would be breaking the law if we spoke to each other. If a greeting passed between Hymie and me, it would be against the law. It was seven years before the two Barsels came to London on holiday, having unexpectedly been granted passports, and I saw and spoke to them again.

The formalities of our release were over soon after eight on Thursday morning. Hymie was waiting in the hallway. He was careful not to speak to me, and addressed his wife instead, but so that I could hear: "There's no one to meet Jean." They were worried about this, but I wasn't. They would take my suitcase with them in the car, to be picked up later, and I would make a telephone call, outside the walls.

I preferred it like that. It was a wonderful autumn morning in Johannesburg, very bright and crisp. It felt exhilarating, yet exquisitely normal. I knew that South Africa was still gripped by severe repression, that extreme cruelty still flourished, that thousands of political prisoners still suffered in various gaols, but, that day, all I was conscious of was the joy of my own freedom, and the sense that the rest of my life would be an adventure. On the corner of Hospital Hill, I bought a copy of the *Rand Daily Mail*. Before I was arrested, I used to buy a paper from that same seller, every morning, on my way to the bus-stop. "Where have you been?" he asked. I told him.

I used a payphone in the cafe on the corner. It was the first day of the Easter school holidays, and Elena and Lucy were waiting at Lucy's house, ready to fetch me. They were surprised to get a call from me, for they had expected one from the Lieutenant in charge of the female prison. She had promised to let them know when I was being released, and, in their ignorance of prison ways, they had put perfect trust in her.

I was proud of my nonchalance. "I'll have coffee while I wait for you," I said, and made my way along the pavement to a nearby cafe that we all knew well. It was the same cafe from which, nearly five years before, I had watched the news of the Rivonia arrests hitting the streets. The coffee wasn't good, but the atmosphere was.

I was sitting at a table in the sun when they arrived. "You look wonderful," they cried in surprise. "It's all that exercise and clean living," I answered. It was true that I was physically healthy and fit, but I knew it was more than that, for there must have been a look of relaxation and happiness on my face that they hadn't seen for a long time. "We won't stay here," they said. "Let's go home and have tea."

The euphoria of that first day hardly outlasted the Easter weekend. The small celebrations, with never more than two other people present, soon gave way to a banned person's narrow, sterile life, dominated by routine police harassment. Mornings were spent taking the bus to the Hospital Hill police station, and signing a book in the charge office. After that, I'd buy a paper and read it in the sun, drinking coffee; usually alone, because my friends were all working. I became aware that I was being watched by a security policeman, the same man every morning, and, one day, I saw the change of shifts at precisely midday. I liked to think that I was helping to drain the resources of the apartheid government by engaging its employees in what was useless surveillance because I was doing no political work at all. Goodness knows how much public money was spent on that kind of thing in those days; no one ever seemed to question the police budget.

When I had been out only a few days I visited Denis Kuny, we had a drink and, in the excitement of social life outside, I quite forgot to report to the police. The result of this was another trial; a short one, and the sentence of a year, of which all but four days was suspended. The suspended sentence made it even more important that I should leave the country soon, for I couldn't afford to make another mistake.

The four days in gaol didn't depress my spirits much, especially as the day of the trial counted as the first day, and the day of release as the fourth, so I really had only two days in the Fort. I spent them in one of the single cells; the wardress in charge – the same one who'd been in charge before – let me have my books, brought me a lighted cigarette from time to time, and ignored the fact that I was lying on the bed during the day, something sentenced prisoners weren't supposed to do. I didn't bother to eat much. When my possessions were restored to me in the "surgery", a few minutes before I was released, I smuggled some cigarettes to the other prisoners.

Within the first week, I had visited the British Consul to apply for entry into the United Kingdom. He told me he'd recommend my application, but entry visas were difficult to get at that time. He suggested I try Canada, but this was before South Africans had begun to emigrate there in appreciable numbers, and I wasn't attracted by the thought of a cold country where I was a stranger and knew no one. I began to spend my afternoons writing desperate letters to people I knew in Britain, asking them to intercede for me. Another struggle with bureaucracy began – offices to visit, forms to fill in, telephone calls to make – when I applied to the South African government for a permit to leave the country.

After staying for a while with Lucy and her family, I moved to other friends, Rose and Wolf, in Linksfield, just over the border of Germiston, and, within a day or two, plainclothes men came to serve new banning orders on me. This time, the house arrest clause was included, and I had to stay in between the hours of six in the evening and six in the morning. I was confined to the magisterial district of Germiston, and had to report daily to the Germiston police, instead of to Hospital Hill. After that, I didn't visit Johannesburg again till just before I left, and that was with the special permission of the magistrate and, during the course of my visit, I had to report to John Vorster Square.

The results of my applications came together in September, five months after I'd been released, and I left Johannesburg on the train for Durban. Exit permits had a way of arriving in the post the day before the planned day of departure, or even on the day itself; it was one of the many ways of making banned people's lives a misery; but mine had arrived in good time. I had a little document from the British Consul, a holiday visa, allowing me entry for three months, provided I didn't seek paid or unpaid employment. It didn't sound very promising, but the consul assured me I'd be all right. Two security policemen had called on me that morning; to say goodbye and good luck, they said.

I also had with me another letter from the magistrate. It suspended my house arrest order to allow me to catch an evening train. It stipulated that, on arrival at Durban station, I was to go immediately to my mother's house, and remain there, twenty-four hours a day, until the day of my departure, when I was allowed to leave the house and go directly to the docks. During the course of that week, I managed to get permission from the chief magistrate in Durban to go to the bank and have my hair cut. I had to name the hairdresser, and the letter in reply stated that I might not have more than one appointment with the hairdresser, and that I must move directly from bus-stop to hairdresser to bank and back to bus-stop. Even the bus-stops were specified.

When the ship sailed from Durban, I became a prohibited immigrant, according to the terms of my exit permit, and the law didn't allow me to set foot in South Africa again. Mail ships in those days docked for a day at East London and Port Elizabeth, and spent four days in Cape Town, and, in port, when other passengers went ashore, I used to sit in the saloon with my portable typewriter, writing letters which I posted in the ship's mailbox. In Cape Town, when the telephone was brought on board, I rang a bookshop – we had docked at the foot of Adderley Street, and I could almost see it from the deck – and ordered a few paperbacks, cash on delivery. A few minutes before the ship sailed, some men who introduced themselves as "plainclothes customs officers" came to check that I was on board.

At Southampton, my little British document got me through somehow; after making a telephone call, the immigration officer stamped it, and said, "Between ourselves, when you get the offer of a job, go to the Home Office." I was in, and on the train to Waterloo Station.

When I had accepted the fact that I must leave South Africa, I had begun to look forward to life in Britain. I wasn't disappointed. It wasn't always easy: I worked in temporary jobs, until the restrictions on my employment were lifted, and travelled on a British travel document until I took out British citizenship in 1985. It was always interesting though. In twenty-three years, I got to know Britain well, became active in the teachers' union, worked in the Anti-Apartheid Movement, and finally, for the last six years of my stay, worked full-time for the ANC, on the journal, *Sechaba*.

The migration of political activists rebounded on the apartheid government, in that those activists helped to build the international movement against apartheid. We wrote and spoke, describing the evils of apartheid, and urging people to support the campaign for sanctions against South Africa: the campaign I'd first learned about from the document I'd put down the lavatory that morning the special branch took me to Pretoria. In the eighties, the ANC called the work we were doing the "fourth pillar of the struggle", because it complemented the forms of struggle being used inside the country: mass mobilisation, underground work, and armed struggle.

During my three years and nine months in prison, I counted every day of my detention and every day of my sentence. Both dragged unbearably. Now, when I look back on them, they seem surprisingly short, because they were empty of innumerable kinds of experience that go to pack ordinary life: locking and unlocking the door, catching the bus to work, walking down the street, shopping for food, cooking it, choosing what to wear, reading the newspaper, meeting friends, meeting new people.

Was there a positive side to the experience? I suppose there was. I learned to play chess and Scrabble, and have since had a lot of enjoyment from both. I did counted-thread embroidery to my own designs, drawn up on graph paper; I'd never done that before, and haven't done it since. Without that three-year sentence, I'd never have studied for a social science degree. Yet I cannot deny that, for the most part, those three years and nine months were a waste of time.

I think the contribution I made in Britain to the South African struggle for freedom must have been more significant than the contribution I'd made inside the country; certainly greater than the contribution I'd made underground. I wouldn't undo my time in the underground though, not even if those dismal years in gaol had necessarily to be part of the package. If I were faced with the same choices again, I know I would choose as I chose then. I don't know how great the contribution was, that we and our leaflets and our discussion groups made to the struggle for a new South Africa, but we were certainly part of the underground struggle then. We were there. I have no wish to change that.